RESETTING OUR FUTURE

Impact ED

How Community College Entrepreneurship Creates Equity and Prosperity

D0109153

What people are saying about

Impact ED

If we want to have a more just and equitable economy, we have to empower more Americans not just to get a job, but to create jobs. The authors of *Impact ED* have developed a clear and compelling roadmap to bring entrepreneurship to communities across the country.
Thomas Kalil, Chief Innovation Officer, Schmidt Futures

Impactful, and empathetic education is more critical today than in recent memory. The dynamic nature of education and society needs a compass to guide us toward a future that is unknown. This book provides rich direction on how entrepreneurship instruction provides a bridge between education today and the workforce skills of tomorrow.
Governor Jeb Bush, Florida (1999-2007)

The pandemic and economic recession have given leaders a great opportunity to work collectively to reimagine the delivery of higher education and workforce training. This book provides a roadmap to that destination.
J. Noah Brown, President & CEO, Association for Community College Trustees (ACCT)

This publication not only captures the stories of entrepreneurs who benefited by the visionary work of community colleges, it also captures the spirit and dedicated actions of those community college leaders who piloted and scaled this work on their campuses.
Jen Worth, Senior Vice President for Workforce and Economic Development, American Association of Community Colleges (AACC)

This book offers a roadmap that provides hope to those of us in the trenches and a renewed understanding of the power of community colleges and HBCUs.

Caroline E.W. Glackin, Ph.D., Associate Professor of Entrepreneurship, Fayetteville State University

Intuit has a culture of empathy and sharing that is reflected in design thinking, which is core to our business, and this amazing new book reveals a clear roadmap for leveling the playing field of opportunity through authentic partnerships, which is what Intuit Education strives to accomplish each day.

David Zasada, Vice President, Education and Corporate Responsibility, Intuit

The authors bring extraordinary experience and passion to this work and invite you into their world where every student has an opportunity, everyone is supported and valued, and there are no limits.

Doan Winkel, Ph.D., John J. Kahl, Sr. Chair in Entrepreneurship at John Carroll University

RESETTING OUR FUTURE

Impact ED

How Community College
Entrepreneurship Creates Equity
and Prosperity

Rebecca A. Corbin, Ed.D.,

Andrew Gold, Ph.D.,

Mary Beth Kerly, MBA,

CHANGEMAKERS
BOOKS

Winchester, UK
Washington, USA

JOHN HUNT PUBLISHING

First published by Changemakers Books, 2021
Changemakers Books is an imprint of John Hunt Publishing Ltd., No. 3 East Street,
Alresford, Hampshire SO24 9EE, UK
office@jhpbooks.com
www.johnhuntpublishing.com
www.changemakers-books.com

For distributor details and how to order please visit the 'Ordering' section on our website.

ISBN: 978 1 78904 797 4
978 1 78904 798 1 (ebook)
Library of Congress Control Number: 2020949701

A CIP catalogue record for this book is available from the British Library.

Design: Stuart Davies

UK: Printed and bound by CPI Group (UK) Ltd, Croydon, CR0 4YY
Printed in North America by CPI GPS partners

We operate a distinctive and ethical publishing philosophy in
all areas of our business, from our global network of authors to
production and worldwide distribution.

Contents

This book is dedicated to the educational innovators throughout the world who inspire students to take risks while embracing and learning from failure in pursuit of their dreams. We believe that achieving equity is possible and that our economy can recover with a community focus on learning, entrepreneurial mindset, and action.

The *Resetting Our Future* Series

At this critical moment of history, with a pandemic raging, we have the rare opportunity for a Great Reset – to choose a different future. This series provides a platform for pragmatic thought leaders to share their vision for change based on their deep expertise. For communities and nations struggling to cope with the crisis, these books will provide a burst of hope and energy to help us take the first difficult steps towards a better future.
– Tim Ward, publisher, Changemakers Books

What if Solving the Climate Crisis Is Simple?
Tom Bowman, President of Bowman Change, Inc., and writing-team lead for the U.S. ACE National Strategic Planning Framework

Zero Waste Living, the 80/20 Way
The Busy Person's Guide to a Lighter Footprint
Stephanie Miller, Founder of Zero Waste in DC, and former Director, IFC Climate Business Department.

A Chicken Can't Lay a Duck Egg
How COVID-19 can Solve the Climate Crisis
Graeme Maxton, (former Secretary-General of the Club of Rome), and Bernice Maxton-Lee (former Director, Jane Goodall Institute)

A Global Playbook for the Next Pandemic
Anne Kabagambe, World Bank Executive Director

Power Switch
How We Can Reverse Extreme Inequality
Paul O'Brien, VP Policy and Advocacy, Oxfam America

Impact ED
How Community College Entrepreneurship Creates Equity and Prosperity
Rebecca Corbin (President & CEO, National Association for Community College Entrepreneurship), Andrew Gold and Mary Beth Kerly (both business faculty, Hillsborough Community College)

Learning from Tomorrow
Using Strategic Foresight to Prepare for the Next Big Disruption
Bart Édes, North American Representative, Asian Development Bank

SMART Futures for a Flourishing World
A Paradigm Shift for Achieving the Sustainable Development Goals
Dr. Claire Nelson, Chief Visionary Officer and Lead Futurist, The Futures Forum

Cut Super Climate Pollutants, Now!
The Ozone Treaty's Urgent Lessons for Speeding Up Climate Action
Alan Miller (former World Bank representative for global climate negotiations) and Durwood Zaelke, (President, The Institute for Governance & Sustainable Development, and co-director, The Program on Governance for Sustainable Development at UC Santa Barbara)
www.ResettingOurFuture.com

Reconstructing Blackness
Rev. Charles Howard, Chaplin, University of Pennsylvania, Philadelphia

Foreword

by Thomas Lovejoy

The pandemic has changed our world. Lives have been lost. Livelihoods as well. Far too many face urgent problems of health and economic security, but almost all of us are reinventing our lives in one way or another. Meeting the immediate needs of the less fortunate is obviously a priority, and a big one. But beyond those compassionate imperatives, there is also tremendous opportunity for what some people are calling a "Great Reset." This series of books, *Resetting Our Future*, is designed to provide pragmatic visionary ideas and stimulate a fundamental rethink of the future of humanity, nature and the economy.

I find myself thinking about my parents, who had lived through the Second World War and the Great Depression, and am still impressed by the sense of frugality they had attained. When packages arrived in the mail, my father would save the paper and string; he did it so systematically I don't recall our ever having to buy string. Our diets were more careful: whether it could be afforded or not, beef was restricted to once a week. When aluminum foil—the great boon to the kitchen—appeared, we used and washed it repeatedly until it fell apart. Bottles, whether Coca-Cola or milk, were recycled.

Waste was consciously avoided. My childhood task was to put out the trash; what goes out of my backdoor today is an unnecessary multiple of that. At least some of it now goes to recycling but a lot more should surely be possible.

There was also a widespread sense of service to a larger community. Military service was required of all. But there was also the Civilian Conservation Corps, which had provided jobs and repaired the ecological destruction that had generated the Dust Bowl. The Kennedy administration introduced the Peace

Corps and the President's phrase "Ask not what your country can do for you but what you can do for your country" still resonates in our minds.

There had been antecedents, but in the 1970s there was a global awakening about a growing environmental crisis. In 1972, The United Nations held its first conference on the environment at Stockholm. Most of the modern US institutions and laws about environment were established under moderate Republican administrations (Nixon and Ford). Environment was seen not just as appealing to "greenies" but also as a thoughtful conservative's issue. The largest meeting of Heads of State in history, the Earth Summit, took place in Rio de Janeiro in 1992 and three international conventions—climate change, biodiversity (on which I was consulted) and desertification— came into existence.

But three things changed. First, there now are three times as many people alive today as when I was born and each new person deserves a minimum quality of life. Second, the sense of frugality was succeeded by a growing appetite for affluence and an overall attitude of entitlement. And third, conservative political advisors found advantage in demonizing the environment as comity vanished from the political dialogue.

Insufficient progress has brought humanity and the environment to a crisis state. The CO2 level in the atmosphere at 415 ppm (parts per million) is way beyond a non-disruptive level around 350 ppm. (The pre-industrial level was 280 ppm.)

Human impacts on nature and biodiversity are not just confined to climate change. Those impacts will not produce just a long slide of continuous degradation. The pandemic is a direct result of intrusion upon, and destruction of, nature as well as wild-animal trade and markets. The scientific body of the UN Convention on Biological Diversity warned in 2020 that we could lose a million species unless there are major changes in human interactions with nature.

We still can turn those situations around. Ecosystem restoration at scale could pull carbon back out of the atmosphere for a soft landing at 1.5 degrees of warming (at 350 ppm), hand in hand with a rapid halt in production and use of fossil fuels. The Amazon tipping point where its hydrological cycle would fail to provide enough rain to maintain the forest in southern and eastern Amazonia can be solved with major reforestation. The oceans' biology is struggling with increasing acidity, warming and ubiquitous pollution with plastics: addressing climate change can lower the first two and efforts to remove plastics from our waste stream can improve the latter.

Indisputably, we need a major reset in our economies, what we produce, and what we consume. We exist on an amazing living planet, with a biological profusion that can provide humanity a cornucopia of benefits—and more that science has yet to reveal—and all of it is automatically recyclable because nature is very good at that. Scientists have determined that we can, in fact, feed all the people on the planet, and the couple billion more who may come, by a combination of selective improvements of productivity, eliminating food waste and altering our diets (which our doctors have been advising us to do anyway).

The *Resetting Our Future* series is intended to help people think about various ways of economic and social rebuilding that will support humanity for the long term. There is no single way to do this and there is plenty of room for creativity in the process, but nature with its capacity for recovery and for recycling can provide us with much inspiration, including ways beyond our current ability to imagine.

Ecosystems do recover from shocks, but the bigger the shock, the more complicated recovery can be. At the end of the Cretaceous period (66 million years ago) a gigantic meteor slammed into the Caribbean near the Yucatan and threw up so much dust and debris into the atmosphere that much of biodiversity perished. It was *sayonara* for the dinosaurs; their only surviving close relatives were precursors to modern day birds. It certainly was not a good time for life on Earth.

The clear lesson of the pandemic is that it makes no sense to generate a global crisis and then hope for a miracle. We are lucky to have the pandemic help us reset our relation to the Living Planet as a whole. We already have building blocks like the United Nations Sustainable Development Goals and various environmental conventions to help us think through more effective goals and targets. The imperative is to rebuild with humility and imagination, while always conscious of the health of the living planet on which we have the joy and privilege to exist.

Dr. Thomas E. Lovejoy is Professor of Environmental Science and Policy at George Mason University and a Senior Fellow at the United Nations Foundation. A world-renowned conservation biologist, Dr. Lovejoy introduced the term "biological diversity" to the scientific community.

Acknowledgements

The year 2020 will likely be remembered as one in which we adapted, pivoted, and re-imagined a safer and more equitable world. We are deeply grateful to all of our colleagues and friends in higher education, government, industry, and the nonprofit world who have focused on co-creating solutions to the complex problems our society is facing today.

The authors of this book became connected in 2015 through our NACCE network. We jointly embraced the research and thought leadership of Saras Sarasvathy, Ph.D., of the Darden School at the University of Virginia, who authored the Effectuation Model for teaching entrepreneurship that we reference throughout this book (Sarasvathy, 2008).

We appreciate the dedication of the NACCE board of directors, currently chaired by Shari Olson, Ed.D., president of South Mountain Community College in Phoenix, Arizona, the NACCE staff, and especially Anne Strickland, who provided support and encouragement throughout this project. Hillsborough Community College (HCC), located in Tampa, Florida, a NACCE member and employer of two of our three authors, has been a leader of many innovative educational programs. Ken Atwater, Ph.D., president of HCC, is a former NACCE Board member and a champion for entrepreneurship and equity. Thank you to Tom Bowman for his creative input on the cover design and Carol Savage for her copy editing.

As our respective states were locked down, we opened up our laptops and began meeting for hours ideating about "How might we...?". This is a core tenet of a design thinking approach to solving a problem. We are grateful to the Stanford Design School and David Zasada, vice president of Education at Intuit. We would also like to thank the many thought leaders who embrace a positive approach to problem solving. Inherent in design thinking is a commitment to empathy, inclusion, and accelerated action.

We applaud the generosity of Stuart and Chip Weismiller, founders of the Everyday Entrepreneur Venture Fund (EEVF). They donated over $1.3 million and countless hours to expand and scale this initiative, giving entrepreneurs a starting point for achieving their dreams. We are deeply grateful for the vision of Carlene Cassidy, CEO of the Philip E. & Carole R. Ratcliffe Foundation, and a lifelong NACCE champion. The foundation has provided $900,000 over three years to scale a pitch for the skilled trades competition that includes seed funding. Our work on EEVF led us to collaborate with John Duong, founder and CEO of Kind Capital, and Joy Profet who serves as Kind Capital's COO. They have opened many doors, showing us how venture capital intersects with philanthropy, which has the capacity to accelerate needed change in the world.

Much of NACCE's growth as an organization over the past four years has been through our robust partnership with Verizon. We are grateful to Verizon's Director of Corporate Social Responsibility Justina Nixon-Saintil for her ability to see how community colleges and Historically Black Colleges and Universities could serve thousands of under-resourced, rural, middle school young women and young men of color. It has been an honor for NACCE to work with the Verizon Innovative Learning program and for Hillsborough Community College to participate in it along with 49 other colleges. We would also like to thank the leadership at Michelson 20 MM Foundation, Amazon, and others who have invested in NACCE and our network of 340 colleges.

We also want to acknowledge you, the reader, who cares enough and is hopeful enough about the future to spend time reading this book and considering how you might take action in your communities. As Margaret Mead noted, "Never doubt that a small group of thoughtful, concerned citizens can change the world; indeed, it's the only thing that ever has."

Acknowledgments References

Sarasvathy, S. D. (2008). *Effectuation: Elements of Entrepreneurial Expertise*. Northampton, Massachusetts, Edward Elgar Publishing.

Abbreviations and Acronyms

AACC - American Association for Community College Entrepreneurship

COP - Centers of Practice established by NACCE across the United States

EEVF - Everyday Entrepreneur Venture Fund

HBCU - Historically Black Colleges and Universities

HCC - Hillsborough Community College

IMPACT - the acronym for this book focused on: Inequality, Mindset, Purpose, Accelerate, Community, Transformation

InLab @HCC - the innovation lab at Hillsborough Community College

NACCE - National Association for Community College Entrepreneurship

UNSDG - United Nations Sustainability Goals

Introduction

Thomas Lovejoy beautifully reminds us of the lessons that history teaches through the tragedy of war and of journeys that lead to 'global awakenings' in the foreword of this book. This book is written by Rebecca Corbin, president of the National Association for Community College Entrepreneurship (NACCE), and two highly regarded entrepreneurship educators, Mary Beth Kerly and Andy Gold, both professors of Entrepreneurship at Hillsborough Community College (HCC) in Tampa, Florida. The *Resetting our Future* series focuses on economic and social rebuilding strategies that can be deployed quickly and inclusively through existing college infrastructure and networks of relationships built on empathy and trust. We offer a roadmap to a future that is unknown but is enriched with opportunity and hope for everyone.

Our journey begins on the front line. That is the place where one must defend or achieve something. In the business world, the front line is where employees are closest to the customer. In the military, the front line is where soldiers are closest to the conflict. In education, the front line is where educators are closest to students, helping them to achieve success in their lives and become contributing members of their communities.

The landscape of employment has changed dramatically. The days of cradle-to-grave employment have all but ended, and the rise of the gig economy has fueled new employment opportunities. This has created a need for educational institutions to prepare students with a new set of skills to meet future challenges. Skills including an entrepreneurial mindset, innovation, empathy, and design thinking have now become as important, if not more important, than teamwork and communication on the resumes of employees joining the workforce.

As community college educators and leaders, each day, we interact with students who are suffering from food insecurity, abuse, and homelessness. We also have students who dropped out of high school, are working two jobs while raising a family, and attending school full time. On the other end of the spectrum, we have students who are dual enrolled, meaning they are earning college credit while still in high school, have the support of their parents or guardians, and will transfer to universities. The diversity of community college students is enhanced further by an older demographic and those students with a bachelor's degree or advanced degree who are looking to be reskilled due to a job loss.

Notably, the combined 12 million credit and non-credit community college students include more women than men, with a median age of 24. Only 46 percent are white, with a diverse number of other ethnicities comprising the other 54 percent (American Association for Community Colleges, 2020).

To educate these students and for leaders to support educators, we need to embrace empathy. Researcher and author Brene' Brown described the four qualities of empathy as "perspective taking, avoiding judgements, recognizing emotion in another person, and communicating and understanding" (Espandari, 2016). In 2019, an expert panel of the Forbes Coaches Council noted that empathy is arguably the most important soft skill anyone needs when entering the workforce (Tait, 2020).

The human suffering and loss of life brought on by the pandemic, coupled with the economic downturn that ushered in job loss and financial insecurity for millions of people, requires a roadmap that is designed from a place of empathy. It makes use of existing assets and practices that can be scaled to restore economic wellbeing to those suffering and provide an onramp to the middle class for those left behind before the pandemic.

The Empathetic Workplace describes the importance of storytelling in establishing trust, which leads to empathy

(Empathetic Workplace, 2020). We have learned first-hand the inequities students experience by hearing their individual stories. We have also seen how they begin to trust each other and us to help them find a better path in life that includes owning their own business or securing a job. For the student who suffers from anxiety so severe she cannot come to the front of the classroom to present her project and the veteran who saw her unit destroyed by an improvised explosive device in Iraq, the path forward is higher education and upskilling.

We have witnessed and documented that education embracing an entrepreneurial mindset, which the Network for Teaching Entrepreneurship defines as "a set of skills that enable people to identify and make the most of opportunities, overcome and learn from setbacks, and succeed in a variety of settings," applies to everyone (Network for Teaching Entrepreneurship, 2020).

Some students are on the path to open their own businesses. Often, our students want to serve their communities by establishing nonprofits. In all cases, doing so changes the trajectory of their family's economic and social opportunities. While other students we have worked with did not take the entrepreneurial route of starting a business, they now have careers in education, nonprofit management, retail, and customer service.

In light of today's challenges, community college entrepreneurship education provides all students with the skills, education, and access to capital that will result in a wave of successful businesses. And, for those who do not start a business, the workforce skills that they acquire through experiential entrepreneurship will allow them to bring needed soft skills to the workplace for more traditional forms of employment.

A bipartisan study funded by the Rockefeller Foundation that included key findings from interviews with community college leaders in various parts of the country documented the importance of opportunities provided by community colleges.

The study concluded that "Community colleges can't expand economic opportunity on their own, but the United States will not likely make much progress on inequality and mobility without the key role played by these schools" (Shaw, 2018).

"So, how do we quickly and cost-effectively reach into our communities, help lift people out of poverty by providing opportunities for people of color, those in under-resourced rural communities, women, veterans, and others? How can we help them join the middle class and build wealth, which may have been denied to them through systemic inequality?"

We believe that the answer is by working together through a network of hundreds of community colleges and Historically Black Colleges and Universities (HBCUs) and NACCE's eight centers of practice established by NACCE that provide training, seed funding, tools, and opportunities to people with limited or no access to capital.

The Roadmap — Data-Driven and Shovel-ready Projects Offered by NACCE's Centers of Practice

This book is our roadmap for building a more inclusive and equitable economy for a future that is unknown. Drawn from our experiences as community college educators and leaders, in each chapter we share case examples, highlight relevant data and research, and explain how these national centers of practices led by community college faculty and administrators are making a measurable impact on societal challenges today. At the end of each chapter, we provide examples of shovel-ready opportunities for individuals and organizations to join us to scale impact, taking a local or regional initiative and expanding its effect by inviting other communities throughout the country to follow suit. The roadmap is inclusive and invites everyone to take action to rebuild the economy and create an equitable and inclusive future for all.

We are living through a transformative age in society. From

the COVID-19 pandemic to demonstrations about equality and justice, the spotlight is shining on the inequalities among people both nationally and globally. This is the time for policy leaders, philanthropists, educators, college presidents, and elected officials to lead by taking action to identify and deploy projects to address these challenges. As Nelson Mandela so eloquently said, "Education is the most powerful weapon, which you can use to change the world."

This book highlights four young and adult students, academic leaders, striving entrepreneurs, and others, the inequalities made more evident by the pandemic, and how entrepreneurial education serves as a catalyst to address these inequalities. It also highlights how shovel-ready projects can be deployed through local community colleges to rebuild communities in more inclusive, equitable ways. Scaling these projects to all 50 states will undoubtedly have a profound impact on the acceleration of new business creation and a secondary effect of upskilling the workforce. The end result will be measurable outcomes to uplift marginalized groups and a positive outlet for social unrest that is rooted in empathy, creativity, and hope.

We are grateful that our paths have crossed with yours. We hope that this book will inspire you to take action in your community. Whatever your gifts, our nation and the world need them. The time to act is now. - Rebecca, Andy and Mary Beth

Introduction References

American Association for Community Colleges. (2020) *Fast Facts 2020*. Retrieved from https://www.aacc.nche.edu/research-trends/fast-facts/.

Empathetic Workplace. (2020). Retrieved from https://empathicworkplace.com.

Espandari, M. (2016). 'How to be Empathetic: the Four Necessary Qualities of Empathy,' *My Healing Cocoon* [Blog]. Retrieved from https://www.myhealingcocoon.com/

post/2016/02/16/the-healing-power-of-empathy.

Network for Teaching Entrepreneurship. (2020). Retrieved from www.nfte.com.

Shaw, T. (2018) 'Community Colleges Offer Key Partnerships for Expanding Economic Opportunity,' *Bipartisan Policy Center*. Retrieved from https://bipartisanpolicy.org/blog/community-colleges-offer-key-partnerships-for-expanding-economic-opportunity/.

Tait, B. (2020). 'The Importance of Empathy in Leadership,' *Forbes*. Retrieved from https://www.forbes.com/sites/forbescoachescouncil/2020/02/06/the-importance-of-empathy-in-leadership/#201867b02d16.

Chapter 1

Inequality—from Reality to Opportunity

As long as poverty, injustice, and gross inequality persist in our world, none of us can truly rest.
Nelson Mandela

Overview

In this chapter we introduce you to the concept of inequality from the perspective of an immigrant student who engaged with Hillsborough Community College (HCC) faculty to learn and to earn a certificate in entrepreneurship and start a business. The opportunity to build wealth is a great equalizer. It is a remediation for systemic racism, and it levels the playing field for immigrants, people of color, and women. NACCE's center of practice focused on equity and diversity has created an alliance of community colleges and Historically Black Colleges and Universities (HBCUs) to foster education, training, and resources. Much opportunity exists to expand this work to address social injustice and inequality by supporting new businesses started by people without access to loans, or what entrepreneurs commonly refer to as "friends and family money."

Case Example

Frantz Benjamin, founder of FB Collections LLC, engaged with HCC faculty to earn a certificate in entrepreneurship and received seed funding to start a business. Growing up in Haiti, he witnessed the effect fashion could have on a person's self-confidence, inspiring his personal passion to design shoes that make men feel unique and good about themselves. At first, he thought he would sell shoes to everyone. Yet, after learning about an entrepreneurial mindset, sales, distribution, and marketing, he realized that Black business owners who had money to purchase trendy shoe and fashion designs often lacked suppliers. He fine-tuned a plan for translating his passion into economic opportunity by filling that gap in the supply chain, helping his own business and others in the process.

"FB Collections was a dream that I had the chance to bring to fruition," Frantz said. "When everything closed in the spring due to the pandemic, my sales slowed down. We learned about pivoting and continually focusing on solving a problem for a customer, so I initially thought of offering body creams. After meeting with my mentor at the college, I realized that I should focus on a foot cream that helped people care for themselves and aligned more directly with my product line." Frantz's entrepreneurial education helped him to start a business and adapt that business to overcome unprecedented economic and social challenges. The desire to solve a problem, create, and give back to others is a cycle that we see time and again with community college student entrepreneurs. While Frantz is a wonderful case example of someone who has been able to navigate racial inequality and figure out a way to help other Black-owned businesses to have opportunity, racial and gender inequality remains prevalent.

Why Is Racial and Gender Inequality Such an Important Issue?

Racial inequality in education, standard of living, health care, and wealth accumulation are well known and documented. Far less understood are the large and relentless racial disparities in small business entrepreneurship. Entrepreneurship has long been perceived as a tool for leveling the economic playing field and providing inclusive opportunity for all, regardless of race, socioeconomic background, and gender. The rags-to-riches aura surrounding entrepreneurship is one that feels appealing and has fueled increased interest in it. While this perception may be true in some ways, the reality is that disadvantaged and underserved populations face far greater challenges when pursuing their own small business enterprise. It is far from the mythological entrepreneurship "success story" of a person who experienced an "aha moment," dropped out of college, started a business in a garage, and rose to success. Some facts about the profile of an entrepreneur paint a different picture and reveal some surprising data points worth mentioning.

A Kauffman Foundation survey found that 95 percent of company founders had a baccalaureate degree, 60 percent were male, nearly 80 percent of the founders were white, and a majority (82 percent) were 30 years of age or older. "The fact that 95 percent of company founders have a baccalaureate degree isn't the only indication of how education plays a role; the Kauffman study also discloses that roughly 75 percent of founders ranked in the top 30 percent of their high school classes, with 52 percent claiming to be in the top 10 percent. In their college environments, 67 percent of respondents claimed to be in the top 30 percent, while 37 percent claimed to be in the top 10 percent" (The Kauffman Foundation, 2009). Because this data demonstrates that in many cases entrepreneurs are high academic achievers, the achievement gap, defined as the continual inequality in academic achievement between minority and disadvantaged students and their white equivalents, contributes strongly to the inequity in entrepreneurial opportunity.

Many individuals from underserved communities, aspiring everyday entrepreneurs in particular, remain crowded out from pursuing self-employment for numerous reasons. As a result, the field of entrepreneurship remains largely homogeneous (80 percent white and 65 percent male).

A 2018 report from the Organization for Economic Cooperation and Development (OECD) reveals that while the gender gap has narrowed significantly in labor workforce participation, women continue to lag behind in new venture creation. According to the report, men were nearly two times more likely to be self-employed than women (Organization for Economic Cooperation and Development, 2018). However, when you dig deeper into the data, you discover that women are more likely to start businesses that address a market need rather than starting a business out of economic necessity. A widely accepted finding in entrepreneurship literature is that new business formation tends to increase during recessions, particularly among the unemployed. Azer Dilanchiev examined the case of Georgia and noted that historically in times of unemployment people turn to self-employment (Dilanchiev, 2014). This pattern has persisted from the 1940s through the Great Recession of 2008-2009,

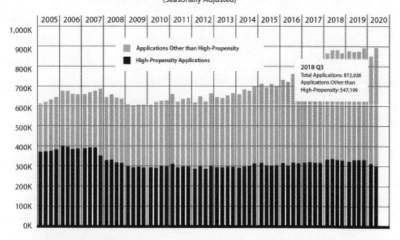

Quarterly Business Applications
As of 2020 Q2
(Seasonally Adjusted)

Business Applications (BA)
All Employer Identification Number (EIN) applications for business purposes.

High-propensity Business Applications (HBA)
Business Applications that have a high propensity of turning into businesses with payroll.

U.S. Department of Commerce
U.S. Census Bureau
census.gov

Source: Business Formation Statistics

U.S. Census report of business applications as of the 2nd quarter of 2020

according to economist Robert W. Fairlie (Fairlie, 2013).

This counter-cyclical pattern is examined by separating business creation into two components: opportunity and necessity entrepreneurship. Opportunity entrepreneurs are individuals who are currently employed, see an opportunity, and build a business to meet the market need. Necessity entrepreneurs are unemployed individuals who are trying to start a business out of economic necessity. As such, opportunity entrepreneurs are more successful because those businesses are born out of market need, rather than economic desperation.

Although, as *Entrepreneur* magazine reports, the majority of business owners are male. When distinguishing between opportunity and necessity entrepreneurs as it relates to gender, we find that while there is some variance globally, women are generally more likely to pursue opportunity ventures when compared to their male counterparts — 85 percent female vs. 78 percent male (*Entrepreneur*, 2018). This means that women are more likely to pursue ventures that have a greater probability of sustainability.

To help nurture more female opportunity entrepreneurs enrolled at community colleges, NACCE created an innovative solution to address complex challenges facing women in entrepreneurship, as well as underserved populations. A national network of centers of practice provides unique programming, mentoring, advocacy, and research to address issues related to inequality, inclusion, and diversity. NACCE and its community college partners are helping to lift those most in need, providing broad access to innovative entrepreneurial education and robust resources.

NACCE Centers of Practice for Community Impact

NACCE endeavored to increase the engagement of its 300 member colleges in 2016. Our idea grew out of a member-serving-member philosophy in which community colleges in a region or state would coalesce around issues facing entrepreneurship education in their community and then work to highlight, solve, and share solutions to those problems. Sometimes grant funding was provided to accelerate the work. Other times, the project would begin, and NACCE staff would work with members to identify funding sources. Over time, with the growth of NACCE staff and resources, dedicated program management, web-based resources, and research, these efforts reached a national stage.

NACCE began working on building a national network of centers of practice that focused on a specific theme. In 2018, an Equity and Diversity Center of Practice was formed through a partnership with Fox Valley Technical College in Appleton, Wisconsin. The following year, Verizon invited NACCE to co-host a policy forum on Capitol Hill, which focused on diversity and inclusion as a way of bridging the digital divide and filling tech jobs. The forum included several presidents of community colleges and HBCUs. U.S. Rep. Alma Adams, D-NC, said in keynote remarks at the forum, "Diversity and inclusion are more

NACCE Mentoring Council kickoff meeting in 2019 to bring rural community colleges and Historically Black Colleges & Universities together

than just buzzwords. They are crucial to our economic progress and should be a way of life for the workforce." (Jones, 2019).

Later that year, with a heightened focus on equity and diversity, NACCE hired Jeff Smith, the organization's first full-time director of Innovation and Equity. Since that time, with support from the Verizon Foundation, dozens of HBCUs have joined NACCE and participated, along with rural community colleges, in the formation of a mentoring council. The council is part of the Equity & Diversity Center of Practice that NACCE operates from its national headquarters in the Research Triangle of North Carolina.

During the pandemic and social unrest in 2020, Jeff wrote a blog for NACCE that spoke to the importance of taking action. "Our members and partners have a unique opportunity to promote healing and reform as we seek to build inclusive, innovative entrepreneurial ecosystems that eliminate barriers to entrepreneurship and economic success for African Americans and other disenfranchised people," Jeff wrote. He provided eight action steps for working toward economic justice and investing and supporting minority-owned businesses (Smith, 2020). These steps include:

1. Read books like *Underdog Entrepreneurs* and reports like the *2018 Growth Productivity Revenues Output: The Business Case for Racial Equity* published by the W.K. Kellogg Foundation.
2. Provide professional development for your staff that focuses on entrepreneurship, equity, diversity, and inclusion.
3. Work with your local chambers to identify equity gaps and devise strategic plans to address them.
4. Join organizations in your community focused on addressing racial inequity and co-create knowledge about how entrepreneurship can provide a solution.

5. Invest in minority-owned businesses.
6. Develop culturally relevant entrepreneurship programs.
7. Inquire about our efforts to support entrepreneurs from diverse backgrounds through our partnership with the Everyday Entrepreneurship Venture Fund.
8. Become an active part of NACCE's Equity and Inclusion Center of Practice.

NACCE also partners with other nonprofit organizations, including VentureWell that published an advancing equity report in 2020. The report highlighted ways to expand equity and innovation (VentureWell, 2020). The recommendations included: conduct authentic outreach; create inclusive spaces; build confidence; engage faculty as mentors; validate multiple pathways to success; and develop a holistic organizational approach. All six recommendations in the report are included in the culture and programming of NACCE's Equity and Diversity Center of Practice (National Association for Community College Entrepreneurship, *Equity & Diversity Center of Practice,* 2020).

In 2020, NACCE partnered with the American Association of Community Colleges (AACC) to focus on gender inequality in the workforce and created the Women in Entrepreneurship Center of Practice (National Association for Community College Entrepreneurship, *Women in Entrepreneurship Center of Practice,* 2020). A number of college presidents serve as advisors to the center, identifying resources and sharing stories about what helped them on their individual career paths. The overarching goals are to: promote the professional development and mentoring support of entrepreneurial women in communities and colleges across the nation; explore and work to mitigate entrepreneurial gaps that women from all walks of life face; and identify and share or develop, through partnerships with like-minded organizations, unique training and development opportunities designed to advance both women entrepreneurs and women who teach or support entrepreneurs/entrepreneurship.

Jen Worth, senior vice president of Workforce and Economic Development of the ACCC, serves on the NACCE board of directors and leads the Women in Entrepreneurship Center. During the pandemic, which ceased most travel and in-person meetings, a group of ten community college presidents and chancellors comprised of women and men from diverse ethnic backgrounds, came together virtually to share stories and resources that focused on helping women from higher education and business employ an entrepreneurial mindset at various stages in their careers. Reflecting on the discussion in her blog, Worth wrote, "In each stage of a professional journey, an entrepreneur will undoubtedly find hurdles to overcome, skills they must master, and take on an inner battle of boldly risking for the potential reward of massive returns versus glorious and potentially public failure" (Worth, 2020).

Frantz, the immigrant community college student entrepreneur, Jeff, the African American innovation and equity leader at NACCE, and Jen, the leader of the Women in Entrepreneurship Center of Practice, share a passion and purpose for uplifting people of color, immigrants, women, and others without access to resources to advance socio-economically through entrepreneurship. They focus locally in states and nationally by leveraging connections and support from like-minded colleagues and communities. People like Frantz, Jeff, and Jen are sprinkled everywhere throughout the United States. Our opportunity is to find them, mobilize and support them, *and* measure their impact.

The Roadmap: Shovel-ready Projects and Opportunities to Scale Impact

The Everyday Entrepreneur Venture Fund
The success of community college educators and the students

they serve can be greatly amplified by providing seed funding to aspiring, under-resourced entrepreneurs who are women, people of color, immigrants, those living in rural areas, and veterans. Husband and wife philanthropists, Chip and Stuart Weismiller saw this opportunity through their volunteer work at the Norwalk Community College Foundation in Connecticut where Stuart served as the board chair of the foundation and Chip supported the organization with a steady stream of ideas and raw enthusiasm. Together, they created a legacy project called the Everyday Entrepreneur Venture Fund (EEVF). By first investing $1 million in four community colleges in 2018 to test the effectiveness of EEVF, they invested the riskiest dollars. Four community colleges were each given $250,000, as well as support to find local match dollars to ensure the fund's sustainability and provide guidance on developing a funding committee.

The mission of EEVF is to support underfunded community college entrepreneurs early on in their business journey, with a focus on community-based start-ups, scale-ups of existing businesses, and the implementation of proven replicable business models.

By early 2020, NACCE's executive leadership team made the decision to invest organizational resources to expand the number of EEVF community colleges from four to nine. The Weismillers pledged an additional $300,000 to support the expansion, and NACCE embarked on a fundraising campaign to raise $10 million to support 100 community colleges that would create 1,000 new businesses. By the summer of 2020, NACCE secured a $900,000 multi-year pledge from the Ratcliffe Foundation to support a pitch for the skilled trades competition and additional EEVF seed funding.

The chapter case featuring Frantz with FB Collections is one of 50 new companies started with EEVF funds. The company is still operational despite the challenges of the pandemic and economic recession. With the EEVF funding, Frantz was able to cover some of his costs and provide net terms to small Black-owned boutiques. "The funding helped me execute my plan and support the resellers, and it helped to grow the business by 50 percent this year," he said. The funding aided Frantz and his business, and it helped several Black-owned businesses he works with, illustrating how ongoing funding can level the playing field.

Opportunities to Scale for Impact

Additional resources will enable the Equity and Diversity and Women in Entrepreneurship Centers of Practice to provide comprehensive professional development that could be deployed nationally through community colleges and HBCUs across the nation. The training would be open to all community members and available locally on community college campuses.

Expansion of the EEVF seed funding to more community colleges and would-be under resourced entrepreneurs of color, women, immigrants, and veterans in the near term would result in hundreds of new businesses that are cash positive within the first six months of operation. The program would be sustainable as a result of educational training, mentoring, and commitment by local areas to match nationally raised dollars. Businesses, revenue, and jobs created would be tracked and measured through the platform Startup Space developed by an EEVF entrepreneur who was mentored at HCC.

Opportunities to Make an Impact

What can you do? The open-access nature of community colleges provides an invitation for everyone to engage in learning. Aspiring entrepreneurs, adult and younger students, and retired business owners can all take part in a wide range of academic and lifelong learning programs. Speak to classes, mentor, or serve on advisory committees. We encourage you to take the first step to change your community for the better by reaching out to your local community college or visit NACCE's website nacce.com/reset and we will help you get connected.

Chapter 1 References

Dilanchiev, A. (2014) 'Relationship between Entrepreneurship and Unemployment: The Case of Georgia,' *Journal of Social Sciences,* Volume 3, Issue 2: 2233-3878. http://oaji.net/articles/2016/2903-1455537612.pdf.

Entrepreneur Magazine. (2018) 'Statistically, What Does the Average Entrepreneur Look Like?' Retrieved from http://entm.ag/w1m.

Fairlie, R. (2013) 'How the Great Recession Spurred Entrepreneurship,' *strategy + business.* Retrieved from https://www.strategy-business.com/article/re00240?gko=c9bcf.

Jones, L. (2019) 'Experts: Collaboration Needed to Diversify Tech Workforce.' *Diverse Education.* Retrieved from https://diverseeducation.com/article/142563/.

The Kauffman Foundation. (2009) *Sources of Financing for New Technology Firms: A Comparison by Gender.* Retrieved from https://www.kauffman.org/wp-content/uploads/2019/12/sources_of_financing_for_new_technology_firms.pdf.

National Association for Community College Entrepreneurship. (2020) *Equity & Diversity Center of Practice.* Retrieved from https://www.nacce.com/equity-and-diversity-center-of-practice.

National Association for Community College Entrepreneurship. (2020) *Women In Entrepreneurship Center of Practice.* Retrieved from https://www.nacce.com/women.

Organization for Economic Cooperation and Development (2018). 5 Ways Policy Could Close the Gender Gap in Entrepreneurship. Retrieved from https://www.weforum.org/agenda/2017/10/five-ways-policy-could-close-the-gender-gap-in-entrepreneurship/

Smith, J. (2020) 'Entrepreneurial Leadership in a Time of Social Crisis,' *National Association for Community College Entrepre-*

neurship. Retrieve from https://www.nacce.com/news/entrepreneurial-leadership-in-a-time-of-social-crisis.

VentureWell. (2020) *Six Strategies to Advance Equity and Broaden Participation in I&E.* Retrieved from https://venturewell.org/advancing-equity/?utm_source=preconference&utm_medium=referral&utm_content=report&utm_campaign=advancingequity.

Worth, J. (2020). 'Bold Thinking and Bold Action: Women's Entrepreneurship,' *National Association for Community College Entrepreneurship.* Retrieved from https://www.nacce.com/news/bold-thinking-and-bold-action-womens-entrepreneurship

Chapter 2

Mindset—from Stuck to Action

To bring about change, you must not be afraid to take the first step.
We will fail when we fail to try.
Rosa Parks

Overview

Entrepreneurship is often misunderstood. From an academic perspective, applied entrepreneurship education is about more than simply starting a business. It is a mindset, a framework for thinking and acting that can empower anyone to succeed (Taulbert & Schoeniger, 2010). The entrepreneurial person's underlying beliefs and assumptions enable them to see opportunities when others see none. Entrepreneurship education is also a training ground for workforce readiness, as students develop and cultivate entrepreneurial skills that align closely with those skills (i.e. problem finding) that employers are seeking.

People from all backgrounds can understand and adopt the practice of thinking like an entrepreneur and begin to view challenges as opportunities to grow, learn from others, and test solutions. The pandemic provides us with an opportunity to nurture an entrepreneurial mindset in ourselves and in our students to help us better navigate the current economic and social challenges.

In this chapter we will introduce you to the practice of entrepreneurial thinking from the perspective of Jason Hendricks, a young African American man from a poor neighborhood. His experience serving in the United States military, combined with his fortunate collision with Hillsborough Community College (HCC) opened his mind to entrepreneurship.

Case Example

Jason is the founder of Forgot or Knot, a web-based business offering one-of-a-kind gift giving experiences for all occasions. Gifts range from video messages, in-person performances, balloons, and more. The concept for the business is rooted in Jason's background, growing up with 11 brothers and sisters in a two-bedroom house in a poor community. "I grew up in a neighborhood where all you saw was drugs and violence," Jason said. "It was tough, but not knowing *my* purpose in life was even tougher. I remember hearing kids wishing for new toys or new shoes because they had so little, and I always wished I could escape my environment and provide happiness to others by making those wishes come true."

After years of people telling him it was impossible to make everyone happy, he found two professors at HCC who believed in him in a space on campus called the InLab@HCC.

At HCC, Jason learned to apply the principles of effectuation, a way of thinking that serves entrepreneurs in the process of opportunity identification and new venture creation. By starting with a focus on Sarasvathy's "bird-in-hand" assets, Jason began to look for opportunities and not focus on obstacles. "Growing up, my family had challenges and not much money for gifts. Yet, I always believed that giving gifts makes both the giver and receiver happy," observed Jason. "This also helped me formulate the idea for Forgot or Knot."

Jason's entrepreneurial mindset helped him to reconcile and regroup. Despite the economic disruption from the COVID-19 pandemic his business is doing better than projected. "My business is helping my employees provide for their families during a time when the unemployment rate is at its highest," he said. The business has doubled its revenue over the previous year and has recently launched a new product for retention marketing. Jason's case is a solid example of a person who has cultivated and developed an entrepreneurial mindset.

What Is an Entrepreneurial Mindset?

In 2019, the National Association for Community College Entrepreneurship (NACCE) published its first book, *Community Colleges as Incubators of Innovation*. In it, Bree Langemo, one of the co-authors, emphasized the need for an entrepreneurial mindset:

> "The world is changing in ways that we could have never anticipated. Unlike the industrial revolutions of the past, the Fourth Industrial Revolution is advancing at a far greater pace than humankind has ever experienced. Given the advancement of technology, the new world of work, and changing job types that will require new skill sets, the need for *all levels* of society to be entrepreneurial has never been greater." (2019, p. 5)

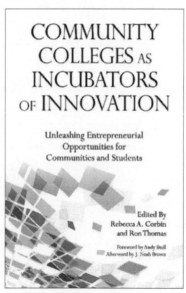

NACCE's first book was released during National Entrepreneurship Week in February 2019

In many ways, 2020 will be remembered as the year that transformed us all. COVID-19 and its far-ranging impact transformed the way we work, learn, and engage each other. As Langemo highlighted in her chapter, drawing on her past work with the Entrepreneurial Learning Initiative, transformation theory includes three phases: 1. Search that includes activities like inquiry, observation, problem solving; 2. Growth that involves management, replication, policies, scalability; and 3. Obsolescence that is driven by innovation, large-scale initiatives, planning, execution, and measured results (Land & Jarman, 1992).

To successfully survive and even thrive amid change and challenge, an entrepreneurial mindset offers a way forward at an accelerated pace because it is empowering and inclusive. *How?* As NACCE has found through its work of piloting, expanding, and scaling numerous projects, an entrepreneurial mindset helps under-resourced youth succeed; it also helps educators, government, and business leaders make better decisions and overcome organizational roadblocks.

Why Are Some People and Organizations Stuck?

Martin Luther King Jr. once said that "Change does not roll in on the wheels of inevitability, but [rather] comes through continuous struggle." It is the struggle to make meaningful change that is so difficult, and the constant challenges changemakers face cause some to cease trying. This in turn causes stagnation to take hold. The law of inertia states that an object at rest will stay at rest, unless it is acted on by an external force. Sull describes the twofold meaning of inertia. One interpretation is simply being stuck, frozen in place. Another application of this term is active inertia, the notion that a person or "organization will simply continue to follow established patterns of behavior — even in response to dramatic shifts." This "if it ain't broke, don't fix it" mentality is triggered by pursuing the path of least resistance. It is easier to deploy a practice that has been previously used than to develop an entirely new way of addressing challenges, especially unforeseen events like a global pandemic (Sull, 1999).

Often, organizational cultures are fearful of failure. Entrepreneurs know that fear of failure can only accomplish one of two things: either stop you from starting; or stop you from stopping. Both are bad and are based on the idea that if you never act on the unknown, you will be insulated from failure. On the other hand, the cognitive bias known as loss aversion informs us that if you are brave enough to try and take action on something and you consciously know the project or business has failed, it is better to keep working on a failed project than admit that you have failed to avoid facing the perceived shame that comes along with failure (Kahneman & Tversky, 1979).

An example of active inertia at work involves the epic demise of the iconic American business, Eastman Kodak Company. Kodak's stock price hit an all-time high of $95 per share in 1997, before the company went out of business. Many believe that the ultimate failure of Kodak was caused by an inability to navigate the troubled waters of competition from Japan (Fuji Film), coupled with disruptive forces emanating from the rise of digital technology. However, a deeper look into Kodak's culture reveals a strong sense of ethnocentrism (the belief in the superiority of one's culture), blended with a touch of arrogance, ultimately leading to an inability to act when confronted by serious external forces bearing down on the company.

Successful venture capitalist-turned-thought-leader and activist Ted Dintersmith thinks and acts in a manner opposite from Kodak. He delivered a keynote at the InLab@HCC's Susie Steiner Community Impact Awards breakfast in September of 2020, held virtually due to the pandemic, and observed, "The process of 'school' crushes out of kids new opportunity and creativity. During times of trouble, we need to do things differently." Dintersmith, an early investor in Twitter when everyone thought it was a dumb idea, added that some of his best deals were the most controversial. As a result of his visits across the nation seeing pockets of innovation that can be replicated, he sees tremendous post-pandemic opportunity for innovation and growth.

How Do People and Organizations Get Unstuck?

It is not uncommon for aspiring and engaged entrepreneurs to slip into a state of inertia. During troubling times, business ownership and execution can be overwhelming and create a momentary sense that getting things done may not be possible. When things are going well, some leaders fall into a pattern of cruise control, which can be equally disruptive to an organization. Business leaders, educators, and students experience this sensation as well.

"So, what can a person and/or organization do to break the cycle of stagnation, and how does an entrepreneurial way of thinking help?"
Amazon founder Jeff Bezos developed a Day 1 and Day 2 philosophy. Bezos argued that for a business to remain relevant, vibrant, innovative, and action-oriented, its culture needed to be developed around viewing each day as the first day of a new business operation. Day 1 of a venture can feel exciting, risky, uncertain, scary, and frustrating all at the same time. These emotions trigger action. Excitement fuels engagement, uncertainty, and fear can promote collaboration and camaraderie. Day 2 businesses, on the other hand, rely on what is working rather than constantly searching for new ways of getting better. Beyond adopting a Day 1 strategy, organizations and individuals can also address getting unstuck by cultivating a "give it a go" discipline and learning to celebrate failure. When others in an organization see someone getting recognized for trying something new that did not work out, that person is more likely to also try something new.

Recent research conducted by a team from the Sloan School of Management at the Massachusetts Institute of Technology reveals some interesting discoveries and suggestions about how to develop a workforce that can leverage entrepreneurial thinking to overcome stagnation and be able to face the challenges of tomorrow. Many organizations "focus on refining the skills their people already possess, which doesn't prepare existing employees or new hires for the business challenges they will face" (Marion et al., 2020).

The Sloan School research advanced several suggestions to help convert inaction to action. An entrepreneurial mindset helps nurture divergent thinking — searching for new ways of solving problems. Many college students today have been exposed throughout their academic journey to increasing rates of test taking, which advances a convergent mindset — learning to select the right answer from a menu of options. This convergent approach can stifle new idea generation and action. According to the Sloan data, another critical skill that organizations need to consider for overcoming the challenges of today and developing a pathway for sustainability in the future is empathy building. Empathy nurtures collaboration, support and encouragement, all of which are needed to take action and break away from feeling stuck.

NACCE Centers of Practice for Community Impact
NACCE's centers of practice embrace Bezos' Day 1 and Day 2 philosophy and speak to the industry need to equip students of all ages with critical thinking skills. The centers are continually searching for new ways to address challenges, and this itera-tive mindset fuels a culture of continuous improvement (Day 1). These centers provide information and training locally, region-ally, and nationally and encourage community stakeholders to take action. For example, community colleges in Iowa are cul-tivating an entrepreneurial mindset in the high-school-to-adult population. In its ecosystem in Tampa, Florida, HCC focuses on immigrants, veterans, people of color, and those without access to traditional capital. Both offer ripe models for replication to reset the economy in a more inclusive and equitable way.

Entrepreneurial Mindset Center of Practice — Curriculum and Effectuation

In the world of higher education, an entrepreneurial mindset is fueled by an interdisciplinary and lifelong approach to teaching and learning. In the entrepreneurial education circles, it is often referred to as the "cradle to gray" target demographics. An early adopter of cultivating an entrepreneurial mindset across the state of Iowa was North Iowa Area Community College (NIACC) in Mason City. Its president, Steve Schulz, is a longtime NACCE board member who came from the K-12 system before moving to community college leadership. Schulz, along with Tim Putnam, a founding NACCE member who runs the college's John Pappajohn Entrepreneurial Center, focus on and celebrate the success of student entrepreneurs.

In 2018 – 2019, Putnam brought all 15 community colleges in Iowa together to better understand and embrace the entrepreneurial mindset approach. The effort began with 13 community college presidents signing NACCE's *Presidents for Entrepreneurship Pledge (PFEP)*. By signing the pledge, each college president commits to five steps:

1. Form teams to focus on entrepreneurship
2. Connect with entrepreneurs in the community
3. Collaborate with industry in your region
4. Focus on business and job creation
5. Share stories through events and the media.

NACCE invested resources to test the validity of the pledge in 2015 with funding from the Coleman Foundation. The summary of the results reported that "with an 83 percent completion rate, the assessment results clearly demonstrated that the *PFEP* had and continues to have a significant impact in the way that community colleges act and perceive themselves as entrepreneurially minded institutions." (p. 166 -167 *Community*

Colleges as Incubators of Innovation, Stylus LLC, 2019).

Following the pledge-signing by nearly all of the Iowa community college presidents, the Entrepreneurial Mindset Center leaders met monthly to explore ideas about how to create a free curriculum that could be shared with other NACCE members. The efforts in Iowa resulted in the development of a three-course series focused on cultivating an entrepreneurial mindset that has been shared statewide. It provides professional development for staff and faculty on student success, business creation, community engagement, career exploration, institutional support, and resources. At present, center leaders are advocating for more statewide funding and support.

In March of 2020, the Iowa center of practice and NACCE leadership joined forces at New Mexico State University (NMSU) in Las Cruces, New Mexico to support high school seniors Aristotle Marangu and Armand Hammer. With help from NIACC and NACCE, the students organized a symposium on rural ecosystem development. Marangu wrote an article for NACCE's quarterly journal, following the successful gathering in which he stated: "Rural entrepreneurship solves problems that communities are facing, which in turn, improves the lives of its residents." (Marangu, 2020, p. 23).

How Does Effectuation Relate to an Entrepreneurial Mindset?

The students and NACCE and NIACC advisors applied a framework of entrepreneurship developed by Saras Sarasvathy. Effectuation is an asset-based way of thinking that can benefit all community members. The five principles of effectuation help guide rural entrepreneurs as they try to spark business activity in their communities. Marangu articulated these principles in a subsequent article published in *Community College Entrepreneurship*, NACCE's quarterly journal (Marangu, 2020).

Bird-in-Hand – look at the resources you have at your disposal as a means to determine next ventures, rather than starting with an end result in mind.

Lemonade Principle – take advantage of the inevitable surprises that come up and turn them into opportunities.

Crazy Quilt – continuously accumulate various stakeholders to help you create a future while reducing uncertainty.

Affordable Loss – minimize the downside of each decision and action, thereby mitigating risk. Always consider what you are prepared to lose before you begin.

Pilot-in-the-Plane – Rather than predict the future, focus on what you can control today and build your future destination.

While entrepreneurship education is broadly embraced and acknowledged as a key to lifelong learning and student success, many early efforts concentrated on higher education and adults. Across the country, many new and innovative efforts are helping K-12 learners also adopt entrepreneurial thinking.

The New Mexico high school students, Marangu and Hammer, had passion and the vision for completing a new project. NACCE had a bird-in-hand opportunity to conduct a site visit in New Mexico and complete phase two of the Transformation of Higher Education Task Force that will be discussed in Chapter 6. This work was affordable and offered the opportunity to collaborate (crazy quilt) with two idealistic students to achieve their dream. If the project had failed (lemonade principle), we still would have learned something. The project, however, succeeded, and we profiled it as an example of effectuation in action.

Design Thinking Center of Practice — an Interdisciplinary Approach and the InLab@HCC Model

The model for the InLab@HCC is grounded in the belief that innovative interdisciplinary collaborations lead to several powerful outcomes for the HCC students involved, as well as lessons learned for participating faculty members.

Community college faculty become better teachers by learning from colleagues in other disciplines. A graphics arts professor can develop design ideas and frameworks by interacting with biology and chemistry faculty. What they learn and share can also lead to innovative ideas for solving problems and creating new products. Students can begin to see diversity of thought as beneficial and welcoming through this model of faculty collaboration. Students also share their areas of expertise with one another. This process allows a student to apply formal learning to practical execution.

Training for faculty and student entrepreneurs takes place at NACCE's Design Thinking Center of Practice at HCC. The center focuses on providing experiential entrepreneurship education through applied college credit programs, community events, and entrepreneurial training resources for military veterans. In addition, the InLab@HCC has a research institute that provides design thinking services to community stakeholders. Interdisciplinary design teams are comprised of students, faculty, and community partners. These teams take on organizational and community-based challenges to design prototype solutions that can be tested and modified. IDEO, a design thinking consulting firm, affirms the benefits of design thinking as "the practice we found most learnable and teachable: empathy, optimism, iteration, creative confidence, experimentation, and an embrace of ambiguity and failure" (IDEO Design Thinking, 2020).

The InLab@HCC faculty have discovered that students benefit greatly from mentoring and advisory services upon completion of the academic program. According to the U.S. Small Business Administration (SBA), the business failure rate is 25 percent within the first year, 50 percent within five years, and 70 percent within ten years (U.S. Small Business Administration, 2016). Students who receive intensive mentoring through various InLab@HCC program initiatives have a significantly lower rate of business failure.

In the first two years of funding, all 14 student businesses started with funds from the Everyday Entrepreneur Venture Fund (EEVF) are still in operation, despite the pandemic and economic downturn. Looking at all InLab@HCC businesses launched between 2016 and 2020, including those that did and did not receive seed funding, the failure rate is slightly under 15 percent, as compared with the national average of 50 percent. This success points to the importance of the support provided by the community college through the InLab@HCC and to the persistence of these non-traditional entrepreneurs. The case studies in each chapter of this book are businesses created through the InLab@HCC. Notably, most of these entrepreneurs are people of color, women, and military veterans.

In 2019, the authors of this book had the opportunity to test design thinking at a national STEM entrepreneurship conference, VentureWell OPEN. We were invited to submit a poster as part of a research competition. Our trio chose to use the principles of design thinking and the thought leadership for the *Community Colleges as Incubators of Innovation* book to create our poster in real time at the event. We offered conference attendees post-it notes and markers and asked them the question: *"How might we spread the thought leadership in our book with a national audience?"* Dozens of ideas appeared on our poster board, ranging from working through state government offices, to hosting book signings through a national network of librarians. This valuable customer discovery exercise helped us promote the book and also win the "Community Choice" award for the 2019 VentureWell Conference.

At the same conference, we led a design thinking session that focused on food insecurity. Showing a video of students talking about their ongoing experience with hunger caused the 40 workshop attendees to connect to the problem and each other through empathy. To teach the instructors about design thinking, we divided the group into teams and guided them

VentureWell Open Conference in Washington, DC where the authors won the Community Choice Award at the poster session

through a process of defining the problem, coming up with ideas that could potentially become solutions, and creating a prototype solution to test. Using markers, pens, and anything in the room to create a prototype solution to test, one team came up with the idea of converting a recreational vehicle into a mobile food pantry. The model of engaging all people to solve problems by better defining them, ideating approaches with other people, and testing solutions through prototypes, is an inexpensive and empowering method of change that can be deployed in education systems, business starts and restarts, and equity work.

Opportunities to Scale for Impact

As a community of educators and innovators, NACCE has embraced design thinking and helped HCC marshal resources through grants from foundations and corporations to create

**VentureWell Open conference prototype developed a mobile
food pantry**

the InLab@HCC. NACCE has also helped all the student
entrepreneurs profiled and speaking in their own voices in this
book to multiply and amplify the impact of the InLab@HCC via
its quarterly journal and in its institute courses.

As NACCE expands its reach, its national centers of practice
are also developing growth plans to scale community impact. For
example, plans are currently underway to expand the capacity
of Iowa's Entrepreneurial Mindset Center of Practice to provide
a curriculum for middle school-to-college entrepreneurship
training that could be shared, adapted, and replicated in 49 other
states through coordination provided by NACCE.

Opportunities to Make an Impact

From the cornfields of rural Iowa to beautifully diverse Tampa, Florida, opportunities to see the world and the opportunities in it through entrepreneurial thinking abound. Community college educators have created programs like the InLab@HCC that didn't exist a few years ago. By working together, the InLab@HCC has created a team of entrepreneurial faculty champions leveraging the power of a design thinking approach. It also galvanized a community of supporters and helped them avoid getting "stuck" by motivating them to take action.

If you feel "stuck" and want to make a difference in the world and are unsure how, we suggest that you look to your "bird-in-hand" opportunities. You can help mentor or tutor a struggling high school or college student – especially now with Zoom and other video conferencing technology. Visit us at nacce.com/reset to find resources, ideas, and a community of people who have become "unstuck" by taking action.

Chapter 2 References

IDEO Design Thinking. (2020). Retrieved from https://designthinking.ideo.com/history.

Kahneman, D. and Tversky, A. (1979) 'Prospect Theory: An Analysis of Decision under Risk,' *Econometrica*, vol. 47, no. 2, pp. 263-291.

Land, G. and Jarman, B. (1992) *Breakpoint and Beyond: Mastering the Future Today*. New York, Harper Collins.

Langemo, B. (2019) 'Leading with an Entrepreneurial Mindset,' in (eds. Rebecca Corbin and Ron Thomas) *Community Colleges as Incubators of Innovation: Unleashing Entrepreneurial Opportunities for Communities and Students*, Sterling, Virginia, Stylus Publishing, p. 5.

Marangu, A. (2020). 'Student-Led Summit Taps Design Thinking to Boost Rural E-Ship," *Community College Entrepreneurship*, Spring/Summer 2020, Pg. 23.

Marion, T., Fixson, S., and Brown, G. (2020) 'Four Skills Tomorrow's Innovative Workforce Will Need,' *MITSloan Management Review*. Retrieved from https://sloanreview.mit.edu/article/four-skills-tomorrows-innovation-workforce-will-need/.

Sull, D. (1999) 'Why Good Companies Go Bad,' *Harvard Business Review*. Retrieved from https://daringtolivefully.com/overcome-inertia.

Taulbert, C. and Schoeniger, G. (2010). *Who Owns the Ice House?: Eight Life Lessons from an Unlikely Entrepreneur*. Cleveland, Ohio, ELI Press.

U.S. Small Business Administration. (2016). 'Frequently Asked Questions About Small Business.' Retrieved from https://www.sba.gov/sites/default/files/advocacy/SB-FAQ-2016_WEB.pdf.

Chapter 3

Purpose—from Partnership to Progress

One of the main lessons I have learned during my five years as Secretary-General is that broad partnerships are the key to solving broad challenges. When governments, the United Nations, businesses, philanthropies and civil society work hand-in-hand, we can achieve great things.
Ban Ki-moon, eighth Secretary General of the United Nations

Overview

As the "Great Reset" opportunity presents itself to the United States and the world, we have the chance to re-create more equitable opportunities for people who were left behind before 2020 and those negatively impacted by the recession. For government, business, philanthropy, and education to unite in this common purpose accelerates the rate of progress.

Using an entrepreneurial mindset and the experience of a successful entrepreneur like Faisel Hoque means focusing on five successful principles of effective partnership: be direct; think ahead; inspire and influence; create a community; and think long-term (Hoque, 2014). This approach of forming and growing partnerships in an accelerated way has worked well for NACCE nationally and the InLab@HCC at Hillsborough Community College (HCC) regionally.

Case Example

Massiel Villanueva and her brother Fernando Villanueva started YÜJ Granola two years ago. Massiel, a yogi with a culinary education, and her brother, an IT wiz and entrepreneur (who makes an excellent taste-tester but whose culinary experience expands no further than watching the *Food Network*), began tweaking the standard granola recipe and perfected their own, making it part of the family. The word was out, and they began producing their tasty granola, YÜJ Enlightened Granola in bulk.

Just as the business was about to launch, the global pandemic struck. Challenges were nothing new to Massiel. As a military spouse, Massiel and her family had relocated 11 times over a 16-year period. She didn't anticipate COVID-19, but she learned first-hand about the power of partnerships.

Massiel and her team depend on the partnerships they have forged with local community entrepreneurs, including farmers markets and small grocery stores, to keep the business afloat. She also attributes her ability to remain in business to the powerful mentorship and advising she receives through HCC's InLab@ HCC. "You have to be coachable and willing to pivot and that's what a lot of businesses are trying to do," said Massiel. Progress for the YÜJ team has come easily in some areas such as branding, marketing, and pure hustle. However, progress has been slower in terms of financial management of the business. COVID-19 forced YÜJ to ramp up its financial management practices, and that was made possible through a strong partnership with a local community college. YÜJ is an example of how partnerships can help mitigate economic challenges and ignite progress, however elusive and difficult to attain. Today, YÜJ continues to persist and adapt its business model to navigate the challenging waters of an economic downturn by fostering robust community relationships and collaborations.

Why Progress Requires Great Effort and How Partnerships Are Critical

Sitting in a jail cell on April 16, 1963, Martin Luther King Jr. penned what later would simply be called a "Letter from Birmingham Jail." This eloquent writing outlined how King saw the state of civil rights in America, and how best to address those injustices. The letter includes a unique passage about partnerships and the relationship between parties. He wrote: "We are caught in an inescapable network of mutuality, tied in a single garment of destiny. Whatever affects one directly, affects all indirectly." (Martin Luther King, Jr. Research and Educational Institute, 1963). As his statement suggests, we are all connected to one another, but how we choose to work with one another will determine the progress of society.

To better understand the power of partnerships and how they fuel progress, we can take a closer look at the "crazy quilt" principle that is part of effectuation. Whether we are attempting to cultivate new partnerships internally within an organization or externally with other stakeholders, capturing the ability, diversity, and strengths of others is one of the most effective ways to accelerate innovation and take on the most complex challenges of today.

The "crazy quilt" principle suggests that partnerships work best when potential collaborators voluntarily choose to partner with one another. When someone voluntarily chooses to collaborate, they are signaling that they also believe in the common goal, and as a consequence will be willing to share their "bird-in-hand" resources, i.e., who they know, what they know, what they have. Stakeholders who believe in the mission are also far more likely to stick with it during challenging times and work at developing innovative solutions.

A powerful example of the "crazy quilt" principle at work is in the highly innovative, diverse, inclusive, and collaborative culture of the craft brewing industry. The growth of the craft brewing industry in recent decades is a wonderful case study in the power of partnership, collaboration, and progress. The industry, while competitive like any industry, is also known to be one of the most collective and collaborative industries of the modern era — brewers refer customers to one another! (Reid & Gatrell, 2017).

A 2019 study of the industry uncovered some interesting findings related to the role of innovation and collaboration on a rapidly growing industry group. For instance, the craft brewing community in Seattle cooperates extensively while continuing to compete actively for consumers. The study offers some plausible explanations of craft brewing's cooperative spirit: "Organizational theory posits that under certain circumstances competitors find it valuable to engage in 'coopetition' or cooperative competition. Coopetition is likely to surface in markets where a group shares an accepted and common adversary, as many craft brewers feel toward large "Big Brew" businesses" (Said, 2019).

The study also underscored the power of authentic partnership and community building and how those ingredients sparked communities of purpose. Craft beer now accounts for somewhere around 12 percent of overall market share of beer by volume in the United States, representing a $23 billion segment in a $108 billion market (Said, 2019). These businesses are very much tethered to their local communities, and as such, forge active partnerships and collaborative projects with local stakeholders. This process results in the scaling of genuine and meaningful impact.

Like the craft brewing industry, community colleges are known for an intense willingness and eagerness to partner and collaborate. As you will see in the following examples, there are numerous ways in which the power of partnership leads to community impact and changemaking.

NACCE Centers of Practice for Community Impact

"Hard times arouse an instinctive desire for authenticity," said French clothing designer Coco Chanel. Whether we are discussing the growth of craft brewing or the creation of high-end apparel for women, disruptions in our lives like the pandemic and economic downturn present the opportunity for all of us to take stock of our current circle of friends and partners. Just like YÜJ and the craft brewers, history teaches us that we must look for opportunity, pivot when needed, and be patient enough to find the right partners who share our purpose. This is most important for all three pillars of society: profit, nonprofit, and government.

Historical Lessons and Opportunity for a National Nonprofit

In 2015 when NACCE was 13 years old, it had a small office in Springfield, Massachusetts with a loyal following of 280 community colleges. College faculty and leaders would gather annually at a conference to share curriculum and teaching practices. It wasn't until the disruption of NACCE losing operating support from its major funder that it had to quickly innovate and reach out to find new funders and partners. An earnest assessment of its needs and assets followed. As an organization, NACCE had a powerful and unique asset: direct reach to more than 2,000 educators and leaders across 40 states. However, the message of "developing entrepreneurial curriculum" was not as inspiring or influential as it might have been. A list of pressing needs for the nonprofit emerged: a rebranding strategy, more staff, and funding. What followed from 2015 to the present was the refinement of NACCE's positioning as a creator of new forms of entrepreneurship education and leadership training and new messaging that focused on NACCE's strengths as a thought leader. Part of that organizational evolution included developing and living by a culture dedicated to continuous improvement and authentic partnering, which has allowed NACCE to broaden and increase its impact, far beyond what was originally thought possible.

At the same time, other foundations and corporations were merging and reorganizing. They began signaling that their future support for NACCE would likely be reduced. This is a reality that all nonprofits need to face, especially during a recession. For NACCE, this offered a unique and somewhat daunting opportunity to explore new models of revenue generation. In response, NACCE created revenue-sharing models with college members, engaged in technical assistance contracts, and, importantly, secured an array of foundation and corporate partners. As NACCE President and CEO Rebecca Corbin stated: "Not everything that we tried worked, but the NACCE board was stalwart in their support of me as the new CEO to be entrepreneurial."

This experience of reshaping NACCE as an organization was both frightening and exhilarating. Organizationally, the experience aligns with the philosophy articulated in the 1954 book *The Practice of Management*, by Peter Drucker, a thought leader in the field of management and entrepreneurship. He stated that in order for an organization to flourish, it must have a myopic focus on creating new customers and new sources of cash flow (Drucker, 1954).

Leading up to 2016, NACCE as an organization had achieved some great successes, but relied on what it already had secured in terms of funding. It was not until the shock of losing a core source of funding that NACCE was disrupted into rapidly changing its funding model.

With each community college across the nation having its own mission and each state organizing its community colleges differently, NACCE had to focus on the similarities rather than the differences. Finding the shared goals and purposes of community colleges such as open access, affordability, and serving more diverse and socio-economically disadvantaged groups, enabled us to begin to see the immense opportunity to scale for social impact. The pandemic, economic decline, and social unrest amplified the opportunity for community colleges to be the catalysts that NACCE has envisioned.

As Soder noted in his research and writing about leadership,

"People in organizations are not immune to things falling apart. Things fall apart for us in the public sphere, in schools, and in the private sector. The question then, *is what role leaders have to play when things fall apart? What should they do? How should they respond?"* (Soder, p. 118).

The InLab@HCC provides some answers to Soder's questions and focuses strongly on developing a new way of thinking through more purposeful learning and encouragement, including the support of a social entrepreneurial mindset. This can be very helpful when things are going well or falling apart. Most people care deeply about the world around them and are excited to work on developing innovative ideas that contribute toward making the world a better place. Much of social venturing is centered around a strong sense of purpose that ignites creative and innovative solutions to myriad societal, economic, and environmental challenges. The social entrepreneurial mindset of doing well by doing good resonates with large and diverse populations like Millennials and Generation Z. Social venturing includes for-profit businesses that leverage profits for social good. Also, nonprofit organizations that adopt market-based revenue streams to supplement traditional funding models are becoming increasingly common. The InLab@HCC is one example of an innovative, community-focused model that can be scaled to rebuild a more equitable economy through social entrepreneurship education, community services, and events that take on societal challenges.

Opportunities to Scale for Impact

In 2015, Rebecca became the leader of NACCE and was working with the Appalachian Regional Commission on a series of grants designed to raise awareness of entrepreneurship among community colleges located within 13 states. The objective was to introduce new empowering concepts to distressed rural communities where coal layoffs, opioid addiction, and other social challenges existed. In *Entrepreneur* magazine, Rebecca and a colleague published an op-ed piece noting that community colleges can accelerate innovative strategies by sharing and co-creating new solutions (Corbin & Schulz, 2017). The article pointed out "that the dynamic West Coast can even learn from remote rural areas." NACCE has learned this working with 11 community colleges in rural Appalachia. Creating ecosystem maps and leveraging community resources in Kentucky, West Virginia, and Tennessee has led to a larger ecosystem-building project in California where NACCE is now focused on creating makerspaces with 28 community colleges. Makerspaces have many names, including hackerspace, FabLab, and idea lab, among others. Makerspaces provide students with a safe place to try new things, be creative, and encounter failure and learn to try again. Most makerspaces include equipment such as 3D printers, computers, and other technology. But they can sometimes house sewing machines, art supplies, and t-shirt presses. When makerspaces are located within an educational setting, mentors and subject-matter experts are often a part of the programming to help students develop 21st century work skills, including problem solving, critical thinking, and collaboration.

This work in Appalachia led to an innovation in California that resulted in NACCE securing a three-year technical assistance grant to work with a large network of California community colleges in the creation and advancement of makerspaces. In 2020, in the midst of the pandemic, this work continues with the support of Schmidt Futures and Citizens Schools. Makerspaces on college campuses are producing protective equipment on their 3D printers for their own colleges and surrounding health care institutions and are learning new ways of working safely.

Opportunities to Make an Impact

Opportunities for collaboration exist in every community and organization. Whether you are an unknown, reluctant, or a born entrepreneur, consider how you might embrace an entrepreneurial mindset to create partnerships in your own community. These could arise from your unique areas of interest or from the needs you see in your community.

In every community, you will find people and organizations like the Rotary Club, SCORE, and others that are pursuing and supporting small business entrepreneurship. A community college is a terrific place to begin getting involved with a diverse group of aspiring entrepreneurs. Earlier in the book, we shared the story of Chip and Stuart Weismiller and their vision to provide access to capital to everyday entrepreneurs. As we work toward scaling that initiative, we are planning to launch a new podcast featuring inspiring stories of everyday entrepreneurs.

Whatever your passion is – capital, subject-matter expertise, a commitment of time and energy, or simply your own story others can learn from – we invite you to collaborate with us as a guest for our podcast, volunteer, invest in a makerspace in your community, and/or to support our ability to scale access to business funding through the Everyday Entrepreneur Venture Fund.

Chapter 3 References

Corbin, R. and Schulz, A. (2017). 'Community Colleges and the Creation of Entrepreneurial Ecosystems,' *Entrepreneur Magazine.* Retrieved from https://www.entrepreneur.com/article/300894.

Drucker, P. F. (1954) *The Practice of Management.* New York, Harper & Row.

Hoque, F. (2014) '5 Principles for Building Better Partnerships,' *Fast Company.* Retrieved from https://www.fastcompany.com/3025981/5-principles-for-building-better-partnerships.

Martin Luther King, Jr. Research and Educational Institute (1963). "Letter from a Birmingham Jail.' Retrieved from http://okra.stanford.edu/transcription/document_images/undecided/630416-019.pdf

Reid, N. and Gatrell, J. D. (2017) 'Creativity, Community, & Growth: A Social Geography of Urban Craft Beer,' *REGION*, vol. 4, no. 1, pp. 31-49.

Said, Z. (2019) 'Craft Beer and the Rising Tide Effect: An Empirical Study of Sharing and Collaboration Among Seattle's Craft Breweries,' *University of Washington School of Law*, Retrieved from https://ssrn.com/abstract=3383742.

Soder, R. (2001) *The Language of Leadership*. New York, NY, Jossey-Bass.

Chapter 4

Accelerate—from Upskilling to Influencing

The world does not care what you know, but rather what you can do with what you know.
Tony Wagner

Overview

For society to re-emerge from the global pandemic of 2020, many conditions need to be created while other systemic problems need to be eradicated. We know that while change is still occurring, it is accelerating at a different pace because of the pandemic. We are witnessing increased economic volatility that was percolating for many years prior to 2020 (the dot-com bubble of 2000, the Great Recession of 2008). This volatility has tended to hit hardest those communities most at risk.

While it has caused many new economic barriers to surface, it now appears that the global pandemic will not mark the end of globalization, but rather propel globalization into a new phase. As the reset from the pandemic unfolds, new skills will need to be cultivated. For this to happen, it won't be sufficient to reform education as we know it; it must be transformed on a massive scale. Increasingly, organizations are focusing on skill capability rather than what schools their employees attended or what degrees they earned. What businesses and groups are looking for are individuals who are curious, creative, and innovative — who are motivated to learn and relearn. This will require considerable upskilling, both of existing employees and future employees being taught in school today.

This chapter introduces the importance of identifying and offering ways of rapidly developing these new skills. Further, it will help influence policy decisions, provide ideas for reimagining education, and give government leaders some ideas about the field of entrepreneurship and how the skills developed practicing and learning about entrepreneurship will become increasingly important in the future.

Case Example

We can draw from many examples that illustrate the power of upskilling as a means for impactful influencing. Dewayne Kimball grew up in Charleston, Missouri, a small manufacturing and rural farming community. While Dewayne now realizes he grew up poor, he did not know it at the time because everyone else was in the same situation.

Dewayne was raised by his grandparents in the 1970s and 80s. His grandmother grew up in the deeply segregated south of Midway, Alabama. She left school after 6th grade to help the family financially. His grandfather grew up in Tunica, Mississippi, and left school after 3rd grade to help support the family.

While raising Dewayne, both grandparents would share stories about the segregated South and the importance for Dewayne to get his education. His grandmother had vivid memories of the Selma to Montgomery march and the horrific events of Sunday March 7, 1965. At one point during college, Dewayne thought about leaving Southeast Missouri State University to attend Selma College in Selma, Alabama. When he told his grandmother, expecting her to be ecstatic, she responded, "Dewayne, you are going to college, but I will never let you go to college in Selma." The wounds of what she had experienced had not fully healed and she wanted better for him.

Throughout his junior and senior years of high school, Dewayne held three part-time jobs. In his junior year, he enlisted in the Missouri National Guard to help pay for college. He started college, ran out of money, and was unable to finish at that time. He became an active duty service member in the Army. During his military service from 1991-1997, Dewayne continued to take college classes, remembering the lessons his grandparents had taught him about the importance of education. He was deployed twice during that time, once to Panama after the collapse of the Noriega government and then to Bosnia. When he transitioned out of the military, he completed his college education, obtaining his baccalaureate degree at Southeast Missouri State.

Dewayne went on to have a career at Kraft Foods, Oscar Mayer, and Tropicana, which is how he ended up in Florida. Wanting to serve veterans, he left the corporate world and joined the United States Department of Veterans Affairs (VA) as a Rating Veterans Service Representative, helping veterans' access and make the most of their benefits. During his ten years at the VA, Dewayne became a subject-matter expert in veterans' benefits, grew frustrated over the processes in place, and decided to retire from the VA. With a little bit of help from the entrepreneurship education he received through the InLab@HCC and its affiliated STRIVE program for veterans, he launched KMD89, a VA Claims Consulting firm to help veterans maximize their benefits.

Today, as he completes his second year of business, KMD89 is growing at a fast pace. While it started as a side gig, it has now grown into a fully formed business. Dewayne's life, like so many others, has been sprinkled with problems, none of which he allowed to overwhelm him. He has figured out a way to blend his informal and formal education to become a rapid problem finder and solution provider.

Perhaps most important to Dewayne is his determination to leverage his good fortune to help others. He recalled how challenging it was to complete college and find the financial resources to do so. Leveraging his success with KMD89, he recently established a scholarship fund in his grandmother's name through his childhood church in Charleston, Missouri. The fund is for young men and women who have been accepted to college and need a small leg up. When asked what the happiest day in his life has been, Dewayne said, "Other than becoming a father, my happiest day ever was the day my grandmother was able to see me graduate from college." Dewayne's story profiles how years of diverse experiences and skill development in the military, coupled with working for large corporations and bureaucratic entities, provided Dewayne with a unique opportunity to cultivate workforce-ready skills. The only missing piece for him was the development of entrepreneurial skills, which he largely acquired through his educational journey with the InLab@HCC and the STRIVE program. The program was co-created with Syracuse University's Institute for Veterans and Military Families (IVMF).

Are Students Workforce Ready?

We can no longer assume that students completing their education and preparing to enter the workforce will have the skills they need to succeed. The global pandemic has only served to magnify this issue. A recent study reveals that a soft skills gap is still prevalent. Nearly 75 percent of employers say that it is *very* or *somewhat* difficult to find qualified applicants with skills and values that are needed by the organization. In this study, employers reported that only 33 percent of applicants possess critical thinking skills; 43 percent have appropriate communication skills; and 60 percent lack listening and interpersonal skills, according to a 2019 survey of 650 employers by Cengage (Cengage, 2019).

COVID-19 has illuminated how much about the future is unknown. By preparing students for a future that looks like the recent past, schools may be teaching young people skills that may not be needed at all. If we are correct that the future is getting harder to predict and the pace of change is accelerating, then we need to prepare students to flourish in these times of flux. Skills like agility, adaptability, creativity, resiliency, and empathy — typically considered entrepreneurial — are just some of the critical skills that might enable today's students to thrive in the world of uncertainty and rapid change (Am et al., 2020).

But, perhaps above all else, there is an intense need to develop an action-oriented mindset. To be able to take action, one must be mentally prepared to face the possibility of failure. Education needs to do a better job of training students to take action and learn from mistakes and better understand and navigate failure. *So, how do we help educate and train individuals to navigate uncertainty?*

One such skill that can be developed and will be critical to a post-COVID world is creative confidence. People have imaginative ideas, but in many cases are unwilling to act on these ideas due to a lack of confidence, perceived risk, and/or fear of facing ridicule. Sir Ken Robinson defined creativity as being a form of applied imagination. So, if creativity is a form of applied imagination, imagination alone is worth little without a willingness to take action and attempt to implement one's imaginative ideas.

David Kelley, founder of global design firm IDEO, defines *creative confidence* as a process of building an action-oriented, creative mindset, and having a willingness to give things a go. As Kelley puts it, "Creative confidence is about believing in your ability to create change in the world around you." The model for developing creative confidence is tethered to a well-established social learning theory called self-efficacy, championed by Albert Bandura (Bandura, 1995).

Bandura defined self-efficacy as one's belief in the ability to succeed in specific situations or accomplish a task (Fitton, 2011). In other words, people with a strong sense of self-efficacy have confidence in their abilities, and as such, approach difficult tasks as challenges to be mastered, rather than threats to be avoided. In contrast, people with a low sense of self-efficacy, doubt their capabilities, shy away from challenges, and are far less likely to take risks. This inhibits fast-paced innovation and a leveling of the playing field in terms of diversity, inclusion, and equity. Increasing self-efficacy among community college students through innovative programs helps to accelerate ideas.

The academic and co-curricular (supplemental) programs that nurture upskilling and prepare students for a future that is unknown can be found within entrepreneurship education. This curriculum, because it is applied and taught by faculty who practice entrepreneurship, promotes active problem-finding skills, functional collaboration, and learning how to operate under intense resource constraints and conditions of extreme uncertainty. These skills empower students to be influential in their own businesses and communities. They may also become *intrapreneurs* — people who develop innovative ideas within their organizations.

As we refer to the model of effectuation throughout the book, it is worth noting that community colleges are rich in resources that can help promote, develop, and support self-efficacy among their students. As you will read below, NACCE has developed a multitude of opportunities that help students develop a strong belief in their personal abilities (self-efficacy), which in turn increases a student's capability to accomplish complex tasks.

NACCE Centers of Practice for Community Impact

Laying the Groundwork for Taking on the Challenges of Tomorrow
From a broad-based network of makerspaces — creative workspaces where people gather to collaborate, create, invent, and learn from one another — to national centers of practice that advance innovation, community colleges are providing individuals with a unique opportunity to safely take action on ideas and passions within a highly inclusive environment. These opportunities enable a diverse group of students to develop a strong creative confidence, and as such, are better positioned to take action on their ideas. This is important on many fronts.

For example, students involved in makerspace learning are taught to be adaptable and collaborate with others as they are challenged to problem solve, improve a design, or to come up with the best way to communicate a project goal to team members. Adaptability, collaboration, and problem solving will be necessary for students to be successful in the future workforce, and makerspaces provide an opportunity for students to hone the necessary skills as they prepare for the future of work.

Even if a student has no desire to start a business, developing creative confidence and an ability to take action positions him or her in a far more competitive light among 21st century employers. We have found in our experience as educators that community college students, many of whom come from underserved populations, are anxious to act on their ideas, but need equal access to the tools and environmental conditions that make trying something new safe and enjoyable. The community college programs discussed in this book all provide a foundational structure for nurturing an action-oriented mindset, and this army of innovators will transform how society addresses the systemic issues of socioeconomic inequity.

One of the many critical roles that community colleges play in post-secondary education is that of a laboratory for innovation. Community colleges are designed in part to rapidly develop, pilot, and test various academic and community-facing programs. These programs are designed to address the current needs of the workplace. Because workplace employer needs are dynamic, community colleges must adapt quickly to this ever-changing environment. As such, community colleges as institutions are typically more nimble and able to implement new programs faster than four-year private or public universities or colleges. NACCE helps accelerate access to resources that colleges, administrators, faculty, staff, and students can leverage for impact. This is all done through the lens of inclusion, equity, and diversity.

Opportunities to Scale for Impact

Woven throughout this book are examples of how people can create new processes and programs that advance opportunity within the community. NACCE's centers of practice are led by people who raise their hands and volunteer to focus on specific issues like workforce development, student success, and other areas that are connected to entrepreneurship and innovation. As we look ahead, we are confident that community colleges will be a driving force that helps shape the future, post COVID-19.

NACCE and the community colleges it represents have and will continue to contribute to the economic welfare of society through innovation and entrepreneurship. The question is: *How can community colleges accelerate that impact? Given community colleges' severe resource constraints that have been exacerbated by the global pandemic, how might additional human and financial capital help to accelerate the expansion of entrepreneurship and innovation through NACCE's Centers of Practice across the United States?* This is the opportunity to scale for 2021 and beyond. The infrastructure, roadmap, and enthusiasm are in place and ready to go. Perhaps you, as an educator, an entrepreneur, policy maker, foundation official, or a leader in your organization might join us in this work.

Opportunities to Make an Impact

Through storytelling and data sharing, we are striving to increase awareness of the myriad of opportunities that exist for all of us to change the world for the better. We can ensure that the devastation caused by the pandemic will not become a lost opportunity to make needed societal changes. As individuals, we have two choices; we can do nothing, or we can take action. If we do nothing, we attempt to stay in our safe bubble and accept the status quo. We hope for better days and for someone else to take action to change educational policies so that they promote workforce-ready people. *However, what if you became actively involved in your community using your talents and "bird-in-hand" resources to help create a more equitable and inclusive environment?* This is how we will change the world together.

Chapter 4 References

Bandura, A. (1995). *Self-Efficacy in Changing Societies.* New York, Cambridge University Press.

Cengage. (2019). *New Survey: Demand for "Uniquely Human Skills" Increases Even as Technology and Automation Replace Some Jobs.* Boston, MA. Retrieved from https://news.cengage.com/upskilling/new-survey-demand-for-uniquely-human-skills-increases-even-as-technology-and-automation-replace-some-jobs/

Fitton, E. (2011) 'Self-Efficacy,' *Funderstanding: Inspiring People Who Care About Learning.* Retrieved from https://www.funderstanding.com/educators/self-efficacy/.

Am, J.B., Furstenthal, L., Jorge, F., and Roth, E. (2020). 'Innovation in a Crisis: Why it is More Critical than Ever,' *McKinsey & Company.* Retrieved from https://www.mckinsey.com/business-functions/strategy-and-corporate-finance/our-insights/innovation-in-a-crisis-why-it-is-more-critical-than-ever.

Chapter 5

Community— from Static to Catalyst

Alone we can do so little; together we can do so much.
Helen Keller

Overview

While the day-to-day teaching profession can be perceived as uniquely individual, the growing complexity and diversity of schools and communities call for systemic change. This can be achieved by more actively viewing teaching as a shared practice, according to Klassen & Durksen (Klassen & Durksen, 2012). In a survey of 5,000 educators, we see the formation of more community schools in the K-12 space. These schools are a wonderful example of adopting a holistic approach that involves educators working with one another, along with other community resources.

This model "rethinks public schools in order to provide children in low-income communities with a high-quality education. It centers public schools as hubs for communities and combines a rigorous, relevant educational program with extended learning opportunities, family and community engagement, and an infusion of social services," according to McDaniels at the Center for American Progress (McDaniels, 2018). This chapter will explore the critical link between working together as a means for addressing societal inequities and how community colleges play a crucial role in this endeavor.

For instance, public school student Kenzie Kleiner had the chance to see how technology can be used to help improve society through a unique summer camp experience at Rogue Community College (RCC) in Grants Pass, Oregon. She was inspired by one of her instructors to create a website for people to post ideas and designs for environmentally friendly technology during NACCE and Verizon's summer camp program. In partnership with NACCE, the Verizon Innovative Learning, (VIL) program is an educational initiative that brings free technology and immersive hands-on learning experiences to help middle school girls in rural areas prepare for the science, technology, engineering and math (STEM) careers of the future. The pilot program was implemented with NACCE and five of its member community colleges in 2017.

This program has now grown to 50 NACCE member colleges via two initiatives: the Rural Young Women program that provides STEM and entrepreneurial skills to more than 1,400 rural middle school girls in 16 NACCE member colleges; and the Young Men of Color program that provides STEM education and mentoring to more than 4,000 middle school students annually. This chapter will explore several examples of how authentic community programs and engagement can help accelerate society toward a changemaking way of thinking, fueled by a "we" rather than a "me" mindset.

Case Example

This example involves the book's coauthors, Andy and Beth. Andy arrived at Hillsborough Community College (HCC) in the fall of 2012. Seeking to spark an entrepreneurship program, he reached out to connect with local community entrepreneurs and met Susie Steiner. They quickly became friends, and Susie began introducing Andy to her network of business owners. Over the next several years, Susie provided the HCC program with the entrepreneurial oxygen it needed to lift itself off the ground. She became a champion for the program and the students, always saying "yes" to help in any way.

Also trying to further build the program, Beth pitched the idea of launching a new event, the "Entrepreneur of the Year Award" at HCC. "Why not recognize all of our community partners by enlisting students in the entrepreneurship program to vote for the community entrepreneur that most helped them," she observed. The vision was to shine a light on one entrepreneur and celebrate the entire community.

By 2014, the excitement surrounding the Entrepreneur of the Year award had grown and student voting was completed. To no one's surprise, Susie Steiner was the top nominee. Beth and Andy wanted the announcement to be a surprise on the day of the event, so they did not tell anyone. As the event approached, they received tragic news that Susie had suddenly passed away. Devastated, they reached out to one of Susie's closest friends who was even more distraught when she learned that Susie had never known she'd won the award.

Susie's family asked Andy and Beth to move ahead with the award ceremony to honor Susie's life and dedication to HCC. The event was filled with sadness, fond memories, unity, inspiration, and above all, impact. It was a reminder that the future is unknown, and how people choose to live each day can make a great difference in the impact each person can have.

At the end of the Entrepreneur of Year Award event, Susie's partner, Mike, approached Andy and Beth. He thanked them, and asked, *"How much money did this event cost you to produce?"* They explained that the event was the result of a $15,000 one-time funding award they had won the previous year. Mike replied, "If you would consider renaming the event the Susie Steiner Community Impact Award Breakfast, I will give you an annual gift in perpetuity to pay for the event and student program support."

September 4, 2020 marked the 7th Annual Susie Steiner Community Impact Award Breakfast, held virtually due to the pandemic. Over the years, the event has grown and become a celebration of an amazing person with a strong passion for entrepreneurship, the power of community, and the importance of not leaving for tomorrow what can be done today.

Without question, the HCC entrepreneurship program would have never taken flight without Susie's passionate support and her willingness to bring the community of entrepreneurs to the college during the early days of program development. It is an honor to continue this award program in her name.

In 2013, Beth and Andy competed in the Coleman Foundation Pitch Competition held during the NACCE annual conference. The entrepreneurship program at HCC was still in its infancy and had received no funding to date. By viewing the HCC entrepreneurship program through the lens of a start-up business, they made the conscious choice to invest sweat equity in the form of volunteer hours to ignite what would later become a national model of an entrepreneurship program that NACCE would seek to replicate in communities everywhere.

NACCE's organizational model was to provide professional development and funding opportunities to faculty who learn by doing. The winners would then form a community of practice that was managed by NACCE. Through monthly calls, the winning colleges would report on progress and solve problems together. HCC applied for and received a $15,000 grant. The award validated Beth and Andy's efforts and launched HCC on a trajectory of growth and participation in numerous other communities of practices with colleges across the nation. The award also made the first Entrepreneur of the Year Award event possible, further increasing awareness of HCC's entrepreneurship program.

Beth and Andy worked diligently on other ways to expand entrepreneurship in the Tampa area. They launched an annual event called the Veterans Entrepreneurship Training Symposium (VETS) to help veterans and their families interested in self-employment. Now in its 8th year, the VETSymposium has served over 1,500 veterans and provided funding to 21 early-stage veteran-owned businesses. Their work with "vetrepreneurs" has allowed HCC to become the first community college in the nation to partner with the national leader in veterans entrepreneurship education, research, and advocacy, Syracuse University's Institute for Veterans and Military Families (IVMF). Together, HCC and IVMF co-created an innovative entrepreneurship training program (STRIVE) for veterans and their families to take action on early-stage business ideas.

Topic Landscape and Relevant Data and Research

Why Does Authentic Engagement Lead to Well-functioning Communities?
In order for a community to go from "me" to "we" successfully, it has to have the right stakeholders engaged. Impactful community building is an ongoing process and takes a long time. In the instance of small business entrepreneurship, the degree of entrepreneurial activity ranges greatly across communities. While support for entrepreneurial ecosystem development has been a popular topic and seems to be widely embraced through economic development policy makers, the effectiveness and outcomes of entrepreneurial communities remains mixed.

The fragility of some ecosystems has been unmasked by the suddenness and significance of COVID-19. For example, entrepreneurial communities with a deep history, emphasis, and focus on financial management as a cornerstone to sustaining new businesses have fared better than less mature entrepreneurial communities that were more about peripheral support such as pitch competitions and co-working spaces. A report by the *World Economic Forum* indicates that the pandemic has caused sources of finance to evaporate, leaving nearly 40 percent of new businesses with three months or less of operating capital, and nearly 7 out 10 businesses reporting they have less than six months of operating expenses (De Cuyper et al., 2020).

We now know that COVID-19 has had an inequitable impact on minority-owned businesses. There were nearly 1 million Black-owned businesses in early 2020. Nearly half of all Black-owned small businesses have closed since then, according to CBS News in June of 2020 (Brooks, 2020). A study released by the Center for Responsible Lending revealed that as of May 2020, 95 percent of Black-owned businesses were not able to successfully secure funding through the federal Paycheck Protection Program, an emergency funding package designed to stave off some of the economic effects of COVID-19 (Center for Responsible Lending, 2020).

Authenticity matters greatly, both in terms of community development and how people feel about work and life, especially in times of uncertainty. There is an increasing volume of research that looks into the relationship between authentic leadership and job satisfaction, according to Buote who writes for the *Harvard Business Review* (Buote, 2020). This perception is also true within communities. The degree of authenticity people attribute to a particular community or subsection of a community (i.e. an entrepreneurial ecosystem), will weigh heavily upon a person's willingness to engage and contribute to that community. Bringing together people is one thing, but bringing people together around a common set of values, interests, and passions can be far more effective. Having one meaningful collaboration can spark a domino effect of enthusiasm for a vision or idea. Such was the case at HCC.

Building communities around shared experiences and people who care deeply about a particular cause is one way of attracting authentic people to the community-building party. Ideally, one of the goals of an authentic community should be to generate wonderful stories that people are eager to share outside of the community itself. Communities can be geographic in nature, but oftentimes are not bound by a specific municipality. NACCE itself is a national model for authentic community-building around entrepreneurship education. The Institute for

Veterans and Military Families is another good example of an authentic national model for supporting veterans interested in entrepreneurship through advocacy, education, research, and support.

The Roadmap: Shovel-ready Projects and Opportunities to Scale Impact

Within local regions, community colleges are providing opportunity, inclusion, and upskilling to many who have been displaced due to the pandemic. Like nearly 1,100 other community colleges, HCC is playing an important role in its community. The community college system serves as a wonderful example of authentic relationship-building and illustrates the strong ties that bind a community together. These partnerships allow HCC to bridge students with caring and experienced innovators throughout its region and beyond.

As one example, HCC has developed very strong relationships in Tampa Bay and across the United States to provide students with a success network of engaged community partners. These partners are eager to assist students in several ways:

a) mentorship
b) educational and inspirational speaking engagements
c) internship opportunities
d) connecting our students to their own networks.

Every community has a community college within its field of vision. Every community college has a rich pool of resources and community contacts that can help support inclusive access to entrepreneurship through experiential education. NACCE is doing its part to help support community colleges nationally by securing funding for unique and innovative programs.

Opportunities to Scale for Impact

As referenced earlier, the largest new contribution to NACCE was a three-year partnership and $900,000 in grant funding from the Philip E. & Carole R. Ratcliffe Foundation. The partnership leverages a three-year commitment to collaborate with community colleges to build entrepreneurial mindset training and business opportunities in the trades and apprenticeships. Through the "Pitch for the Trades" annual competition, winners have the chance to implement their programs and seed the creation of new businesses via NACCE's Everyday Entrepreneur Venture Fund (EEVF), a model that matches all national dollars with local dollars to maintain the sustainability of the program. The goal of EEVF is to foster entrepreneurship and provide funding otherwise not available to start-ups and scale-ups with an eye towards innovation, diversity, inclusion, and local economic growth. To foster that growth, the InLab@HCC plays a key leadership role in EEVF. The HCC staff shares best practices and provides training and mentoring to the new cohort of schools involved in the second phase of the program. Members of NACCE's leadership team, the InLab@HCC team, and the founders of EEVF meet weekly to ideate and plan for the expansion.

One of the business owners mentored at HCC is David Ponraj, the founder and CEO of Startup Space. Educated and trained as an engineer, David launched his business and received guidance and support from the InLab@HCC. He provided pro bono services to the lab to test Startup Space proof of concept for measuring business revenue, jobs created, and the connections among the entrepreneurs. With the successful proof of concept completed, NACCE hired Startup Space to conduct a pilot program tracking the progress of ten community colleges and the businesses they were creating, along with other metrics. By the fall of 2020, NACCE moved out of the pilot phase with Startup Space and began building an online super hub to capture more metrics.

The insights gleaned by Startup Space enabled the college to tell the story of projects from a data perspective. Capturing information about the types of companies served, demographics, revenue, jobs created, and the number of hours invested with mentoring, allows us to demonstrate to potential and current funders the impact of the services we offer our students. It also encourages data-driven decision making and storytelling, while at the same time creating efficiencies by centralizing the multitude of entrepreneurial programs and services offered on a single platform. Aggregating this data and the participating colleges involved also advances the movement from "me" to "we" and fosters greater collaboration across the colleges.

This work has never been more important than it is today with the national and global crisis at hand. NACCE is working diligently to raise additional funds to support these colleges in their efforts and provide matching dollars for their local communities.

Opportunities to Make an Impact

All communities have veterans, unfilled jobs, and people who could learn a skilled trade at a community college or cultivate an entrepreneurial mindset and become an entrepreneur. Business owners who need skilled employees quickly and don't currently have a relationship with a community college can reach out to their local community college by searching online for customized training or continuing education programs. They can also visit nacce.com/roadmap and submit an information request. Foundations and government entities can also support community competitions like the Ratcliffe Pitch for the Skilled Trades.

Moving from "me" to "we" helps the giver just as much or more than the receiver. Young adult children, family members, the elderly, or neighbors who feel disconnected due to the challenges of COVID-19, can seek connection through their local community college. Community colleges serve a wide array of individuals, including those without high school diplomas and those with advanced degrees, many seeking information or new ways of thinking.

Chapter 5 References

Brooks, K. (2020) '40% of Black-Owned Businesses not Expected to Survive the Coronavirus,' *CBS News*. Retrieved from https://www.cbsnews.com/news/black-owned-busineses-close-thousands-coronavirus-pandemic/.

Buote, V. (2020) 'Most Employees Feel Authentic at Work, But it Can Take a While,' *Harvard Business Review*. Retrieved from https://hbr.org/2016/05/most-employees-feel-authentic-at-work-but-it-can-take-a-while.

Center for Responsible Lending. (2020) *The Paycheck Protection Program Continues to be Disadvantageous to Smaller Businesses, Especially Businesses Owned by People of Color and the Self-Employed.* Retrieved from https://www.responsiblelending.org/sites/default/files/nodes/files/research-publication/crl-cares-act2-smallbusiness-apr2020.pdf?mod=article_inline.

De Cuyper, L., Kucukkeles, B. and Reuben, R. (2020). 'Discovering the real impact of COVID-19 on entrepreneurship,' *World Economic Forum*. Retrieved from https://www.weforum.org/agenda/2020/06/how-covid-19-will-change-entrepreneurial-business/.

Klassen, Robert and Durksen, Tracy. (2012) 'Teachers Working Together: Why Collaboration Really Matters,' *Alberta Teachers' Association Magazine*. Retrieved from https://www.researchgate.net/publication/263880909_Teachers_working_together_Why_collaboration_really_matters.

McDaniels, A. (2018) 'Building Community School Systems,' *Center for American Progress*. Retrieved from https://www.americanprogress.org/issues/education-k-12/reports/2018/08/22/454977/building-community-schools-systems/.

Chapter 6

Transformation—from Trial to Expansion—Pilot to Scale

The only way to get people to work on big, risky things – audacious ideas – and have them run at all the hardest parts of the problem first, is if you make that the path of least resistance for them. At Google X we work hard to make it safe to fail.
Astro Teller

Overview

To navigate the troubled and complex waters of testing and expanding ideas, several ingredients need to be present. Perhaps the most prominent is a cultural system that celebrates failure. It turns out that most project ideas fail either because they are simply not good ideas, or the outcomes are not achieved. A breakdown of project data as reported by *Forbes* from Smartsheet found that 35 percent of projects fail outright, 38 percent miss timelines, and 34 percent fail to finish within budget (*Forbes*, 2018). As a consequence, in order to have a successful pilot project, and ultimately one that can be scaled, someone has to be willing to take the reins of leading the project. A culture that celebrates failure experiences the fastest rates of innovation and project scalability. Developing a culture that encourages others to try is a necessity to pilot and scale programs.

One of the reasons to pilot a program initiative is to learn. Learn what works, learn what does not work, learn what needs to be modified, learn about new challenges, and also learn whether something can be scaled to have greater impact. There are times when testing a concept that the impact is high, but the potential for rapid deployment and growth does not exist or is too costly. In those instances, while the program should not advance, efficiencies are created by not pursuing something that lacks potential for high impact.

In this chapter you will read about case examples of how testing trial and error led to expansion. You will learn why it is critical to develop a culture that supports a safe environment that encourages people to rigorously test and modify a project or business. We will begin with a story about a student who came into a community college entrepreneurship program with a business idea, learned about iterative design, and 15 months later is experiencing rapid growth.

Case Example

It was clear from the first day of class that Dana Swenson was not comfortable as a student. She was shy, timid, and a little older than her classmates. Prior to attending Hillsborough Community College (HCC), Dana had dropped out of high school and earned her GED at a technical college. She worked as an administrative assistant and eventually managed a local UPS store. She tried going back to college, but didn't know what she ultimately wanted to do, so she dropped out.

After meeting her husband Doug, a handyman and a residential remodeler, she began learning about certain aspects of his work. From painting to laying tile, she was continually learning about the remodeling business. Doug was in business with a friend of his, but unfortunately, things were not working as well as he had hoped. Dana urged Doug to go out on his own and open his own business. Doug made a deal with her: if she went back to college and earned her degree, he would leave the current business and open his own residential construction company.

Dana went back to school and enrolled in the Business Development and Entrepreneurship Certificate program at HCC. Dana reflected, "I was unsure of myself and I didn't know what to expect." She was balancing working with Doug, raising a family, and pursuing her studies full-time. She was dedicated to learning and took advantage of every opportunity presented. From networking events to customer discovery, Dana absorbed all that she learned and transformed into an entrepreneur. When she realized what was possible and was given the tools to make it happen, she blossomed, and her husband did as well.

Dana and Doug opened Swenson's Renovations and Repairs during the 16-week entrepreneurship program. They benefited from the college's Everyday Entrepreneur Venture Fund (EEVF) that allowed them to expand the business, which is now growing substantially.

"I wanted to be a good example for my kids," said Dana. "You are never stuck in the same thing forever; you can always change and do what you dreamed."

For 2020, Swenson's Renovations has experienced significant revenue growth of nearly 150 percent year over year and has expanded its workforce by hiring four new employees. Dana is a wonderful example of a person who has transformed from a student to an entrepreneur who has effectively transformed a business idea into reality. Together, she and her husband Doug converted that idea into a rapidly growing business with endless possibilities for impact.

How Do We Effectively Transform?

Effective transformational change is an iterative process that requires significant trial and error, with a dash of serendipity sprinkled in. Whether it's transformation in research, education, business, or personal and societal transformation, one thing is certain: the process of transformation is complex, difficult at times, messy, and often can take longer than expected. We have referenced the model of effectuation throughout this book, and the "pilot-in-the-plane" principle addresses the fact that we cannot control the future. Because the future is unknown, it makes it nearly impossible to manage the process of transformation from start to finish. Instead, you have to accept that leading in a transformational way or creating societal transformation requires that you have no predetermined goals, but rather a commitment to learn through trial and error, as noted by the Change Leaders Network (Anderson & Anderson, n.d.).

The global pandemic of 2020 has brought to light the image of organic transformation, a form of significant change that occurs naturally in reaction to a low frequency, high-impact event. We see a form of this occur in a somewhat haphazard fashion through legislation that attempts to address an unexpected disturbance. But organic transformation occurs through a process of voluntary, not mandated cooperation, and because of that spirit, organic transformation can be more effective and sustainable. Take food for example. There was already a growing trend toward healthier eating habits pre-COVID, but the pandemic has accelerated organic transformation around how we eat, where we eat, what we eat, and with whom we share a meal. Thus far, during the pandemic, 85 percent of Americans have indicated that they have changed their food habits, according to Murphy at MDLinx (Murphy, 2020).

The education field has experienced massive organic transformation during the COVID-19 pandemic. Parents and caregivers have become quasi educators and tutors. Formal educators have developed new ways of engaging with students in a digital world. Education is slowly changing from a culture of teaching to one of learning, observed Geoff Spencer who writes for *Microsoft Asia* (Spencer, 2020). Supporting meaningful organic transformation within the field of education are associations like NACCE.

NACCE Centers of Practice for Community Impact
NACCE set a course for transformation beginning in 2015 by expanding the representation of its board of directors and staff to reflect diversity in all forms — ethnic, gender, geographic,

and in other forms. With the vision of better using technology and creating fresh tools, new partnerships were formed. By 2017, NACCE expanded the number of its partnerships with foundations and social enterprise organizations and provided funding awards that enabled a large number of NACCE colleges and their communities to create new resources and initiatives that stimulated entrepreneurship. This overarching effort spanned these areas:

- STEM e-ship programs
- Professional development training
- Rural entrepreneurial ecosystem development with community colleges and K-12 partners
- Creation of new, vibrant makerspaces.

The Roadmap: Shovel-ready Projects and Opportunities to Scale Impact

Between 2015 and 2020, HCC and the InLab@HCC focused on student success in the area of entrepreneurship across all academic disciplines. They accomplished this by breaking down silos and forming relationships among faculty that focused on transforming and empowering students to have a meaningful impact on the world. NACCE has partnered with the Everyday Entrepreneur Venture Fund to address one of the most urgent needs of our country – that of supporting local economies via entrepreneurship.

Opportunities to Scale for Impact

We introduced you to Chip and Stuart Weismiller at the beginning of the book. They founded the Everyday Entrepreneur Venture Fund as a legacy project and a way of providing opportunity to people who don't have access to traditional capital. You have gotten to know many of these everyday entrepreneurs who launched their businesses with the support and mentoring offered at the InLab@HCC.

Another attribute of an everyday entrepreneurial venture is having a "scale-up mindset." A scale-up mindset means that you have an ambition to grow your business over time, and you are committed to actively pursuing that ambition by having an action orientation. Other examples of everyday entrepreneurs in the service sector might be a small law practice that plans to grow by specializing, or an architecture firm with ambitions to grow by offering environmentally sensitive design projects. Small and Medium Enterprises (SMEs) tend to become profitable much faster than Innovation Driven Enterprises (IDEs) and can create jobs and contribute to the local economy much faster.

The owners, subcontractors, and consultants in conventional, mainstream businesses are the engine that drives local communities. Some examples include daycare centers, delis, yoga studios, dry cleaners, bookkeepers, personal trainers, home nursing caregivers, house maintenance and lawn care services, and IT services.

Beginning in 2017, EEVF selected four community colleges to engage in the first phase of its pilot program. Each community college received grant funds to provide seed funding for community-based business start-ups that were administered by the college's foundation. Each college was encouraged to solicit additional funds from local corporations and individual donors to create a sustainable grant pool.

As of January 2020, EEVF Phase I has launched 45 businesses with a total of $596,505 expended through student grants or loans at the discretion of Phase I pilot college funding committees. In June of 2020, amid the pandemic and economic downturn, NACCE welcomed five new community colleges from across the nation to participate in the two-year EEVF Phase II.

Building on the success of the first phase of the EEVF that leveraged existing academic resources, spurred local matching dollars, and created new everyday businesses, NACCE staff set a summer fundraising goal of $300,000. By the end of July of 2020, an additional $1.3 million was raised for the effort.

The $1.3 million included a multi-year grant from the Ratcliffe Foundation, an additional gift from the Weismillers, and another contribution from Clinton Day, a longtime member and NACCE champion. The cultivation of additional gifts from foundations and corporations is ongoing and expected to yield an additional million dollars by the first quarter of 2021. The funds raised are awarded to the participating nine colleges in the program. The colleges secure a dollar-for-dollar match to the national gift, and the total pool of funding supports grants to everyday would-be entrepreneurs identified and supported at community colleges. The brilliance of this model is that it is sustainable and less than 10 percent of the funding is used for administrative costs by NACCE and colleges in the program.

On the equity and diversity front, EEVF founders reported that in Phase 1 of the pilot, the newly created businesses are 57 percent minority, 81 percent women, and 52 percent minority women businesses. In the case of the InLab@HCC's 14 newly created businesses, 53 percent are veteran-owned, 27 percent are Black-owned, 20 percent are Hispanic-owned, and 47 percent (included in the other categories) are women-owned. As of September 2020, some of the businesses are flourishing and some are struggling but are still operational. In addition, all 14 businesses have demonstrated the ability to rapidly adjust to COVID-19 and the economic downturn.

The economic impact of COVID-19 on small business inequality has been magnified. Of the total Paycheck Protection Plan (PPP), only seven percent of the $30 billion was distributed through smaller community banks and Community Development Financial Institutions (CDFIs) (Center for Responsible Lending, 2020). These financial institutions serve small businesses most in need.

To address this inequity, NACCE has launched a national

pilot to provide unique sources of funding for everyday entrepreneurs, typically excluded from traditional funding opportunities. These high propensity businesses have or are tracking toward being cash-flow positive within the first six months of operation. In Phase I of the EEVF pilot, over 50 businesses received funding and were launched. The average EEVF funding award is $8,000. Examples of newly created businesses include shoe, accessory and clothing design/ manufacturing, granola, automotive manufacturers, home renovation and construction companies, yoga and wellness studios, design firms, travel agencies, and a theater company that pivoted to providing police training during the pandemic.

As of September 30, 2020, the EEVF pilot, with a total of 50 companies from four different community colleges were awarded approximately $403,000 in either grants or loans and have generated approximately $400,000 in revenue. Phase II of the pilot is currently in process with five new colleges on board. Several have already received their matching funds and have students in the pipeline to apply.

Opportunities to Make an Impact

By August of 2109, NACCE's first book, *Community College of Incubators of Innovation* was featured at numerous national conferences and opened the door for a high-level task force on Equity and Workforce Innovation held at Tallahassee Community College (TCC). It featured faculty leadership teams from Hillsborough Community College and a carefully selected group of leaders from higher education, private industry, philanthropy, and government sectors from throughout the country. Together, they reviewed key data and created a new model for transforming higher education.

Eight prototypes emerged as a result of the task force's design thinking activity. The ideas ranged from community colleges providing industry-funded tuition waivers through which students could pursue education for high-demand jobs, to partnering with local public-school districts to auto enroll students aging out of the foster care system.

Transforming Higher Education Taskforce meeting in August 2019 at Tallahassee Community College Innovation Center.
Photo: Brittany Clark

Both ideas were brought back to the Design Thinking Center of Practice for teams to work on and begin moving forward. The automatic enrollment concept emerged from a disconnect between high school completion and college enrollment. It specifically targets students who are aging out of foster care because they do not have a parent advocate to help them navigate the enrollment process. Instead of electing to attend college, these students would be automatically enrolled at the community college after graduation from high school. They would receive a letter of acceptance and be prompted to schedule their classes. Of course, they can opt not to attend, but all of the processes of enrolling are eliminated for this specific group of students. The prototypes from the task force will be initially implemented in Florida and lead the way for a national movement.

Chapter 6 References

Anderson, D. and Anderson, L. A. (n.d.) 'What is Transformation, and Why Is It So Hard to Manage?,' *Change Leaders Network.* https://changeleadersnetwork.com/free-resources/what-is-transformation-and-why-is-it-so-hard-to-manage#:~:text=Transformation%2C%20however%2C%20is%20far%20more,bound%20and%20linear%20project%20plans.

Center for Responsible Lending. (2020) *The Paycheck Protection Program Continues to be Disadvantageous to Smaller Businesses, Especially Businesses Owned by People of Color and the Self-Employed.* Retrieved from https://www.responsiblelending.org/sites/default/files/nodes/files/research-publication/crl-cares-act2-smallbusiness-apr2020.pdf?mod=article_inline.

Forbes. (2018) *Why a Third of Enterprise Projects Fail – And The Tools That Can Spell Success.* Retrieved from https://www.forbes.com/sites/smartsheet/2018/11/14/why-a-third-of-enterprise-projects-fail--and-the-tools-that-can-spell-success/#7593f9a116ed.

Murphy, J. (2020) 'How COVID-19 Changed How Americans Eat,' *MDLinx.* Retrieved from https://www.mdlinx.com/article/how-covid-19-has-changed-how-americans-eat/7m3f7Ek2uPtTIYOgAUWkvT.

Spencer, G. (2020) 'Schools After COVID-19: From a Teaching Culture to a Learning Culture,' *Microsoft Stories Asia.* Retrieved fromhttps://news.microsoft.com/apac/features/technology-in-schools-from-a-teaching-culture-to-a-learning-culture/.

Conclusion

Where Do We Go from Here? To 50 States and 50 Nations!

Our journey in this book ends with our arms wide open to embracing all who want to deepen their individual or organizational impact locally, regionally, nationally, and globally. We believe that entrepreneurship in all forms can be inclusive and propel people who have been left behind into better, more stable lives. We are also convinced that telling the stories of people like Jason, Frantz, Massiel, and Dewayne and the other community college students and faculty that you met in this book will inspire you to see the entrepreneur in yourself.

In September of 2019, NACCE was hired by Los Rios Community College District to conduct a two-day Go Global Boot Camp in Sacramento, California. The USDA funded the project through which faculty and student teams worked together to develop a pitch for an agricultural product to export to another country. Through the NACCE Institute, we created a workshop that was delivered to mostly international students and faculty. Students conducted research on what exports from the United States would align with the culture and tastes of other countries.

It was through this project that Rebecca Corbin, one of the co-authors of this book, met Sam Driggers, a collaborator on the Go Global Boot Camp project. Growing up in a military family, traveling the world, and being a product of a community college education, Sam shared what he thought about *Global Flows in Digital Age*, a report published in 2014 by the McKinsey Global Institute (Manyika et al., 2014). "The report speaks to the interconnected nature and flow of goods and services at levels not conceived a generation earlier. It also shows that disconnected communities face challenges when seeking to kick-start economic growth activities," Sam said. "COVID-19 has revealed the clearest local-to-global links between hyper-connected urban areas like New York and Los Angeles, which were temporarily paralyzed by outbreaks, while smaller areas or rural communities initially felt little impact, sometimes even wondering if the virus was real," he added.

With pandemic-induced budget cuts forcing difficult choices ahead in areas of programming to his state's community college system, Sam sees opportunity to collaborate with NACCE in creating a new resource for fostering those all-important cross-border connections and understanding through entrepreneurship. This is the spirit of our NACCE members and the entrepreneurial mindset that we introduced you to in this book.

The Go Global Boot Camp and discussions with Sam led us to see an emerging opportunity for impact that launched during Global Entrepreneurship Week November 16 – 22, 2020. NACCE will soon open its ninth center of practice devoted to global entrepreneurship. With member engagement from across the United States, NACCE will expand boot camp offerings and resources to help community college faculty and would-be entrepreneurs better understand global export opportunities.

In mid-October of 2020, NACCE held a hybrid Leadership Summit in Nashville, Tennessee. Leaders from across the nation shared their experiences about how they pivoted and adapted to the pandemic and economic recession. Many comments centered on the unintended upside of the opportunity to bring people throughout the country and the world together via technology that was not available a decade ago. During the summit, Mary Rossi, director of the Global Thinking Foundation, expressed her heartfelt desire to transform the world by tackling United Nations Sustainability Development Goals four, five and eight that focus on quality education, gender equality, and decent work and economic growth, respectively.

NACCE's Global Center of Practice will work with

stakeholders in the United States and around the world to open doors for all through entrepreneurship. With an unknown future, we are brashly optimistic that providing organized resources will accelerate the pace through which people and communities can empower themselves through entrepreneurship. We invite everyone to join us on this journey.

For Sam, the three of us who wrote this book, and the dozens of people who allowed us to share their stories, COVID-19 may have disrupted our lives, businesses, and educational systems; however, it has forced all of us to innovate and change. This change can be scaled in 50 states and ultimately 50 nations. We believe that the roadmap in this book and the action you will take to make an impact in your community will change the world for the better and allow us to collectively reset, restart, and usher in a new age of equity and global understanding that is rooted in our unity as people and not in our differences.

At the start of this book, we stated "Whatever your gifts, our nation and the world need them. The time to act is now." It is our hope that we have inspired you to help co-create a future that is unknown. We believe that everyone is a changemaker and is born with an entrepreneurial spirit. This book was designed to reignite your desire and your passion to make a difference, and we have tried to provide you with various ways to do so. We have presented several case examples of how everyday people's lives have been altered in a profound way because of their connectivity to the community college system. We have shared case examples of shovel-ready projects developed through NACCE that are at the starting gate of scalability and ready to impact communities locally and globally.

What then is our call to action? We are asking you, the reader, to reflect on your own gifts, your "bird-in-hand," and connect with us through our book website to share your ideas for positive impact and changemaking. We also hope that one of our ideas or stories has inspired you to become part of our community of impact changemakers. We challenge you to join our "crazy quilt," which embodies an alliance between impassioned and authentic collaborators. Every partner is represented as a unique piece of cloth, each possessing critically important gifts.

The true power to make change resides in the binding together of these independent pieces of cloth into a quilt that symbolizes a deep commitment each partner has with each other. In 2019, Dave Zasada, vice president for Education and Corporate Responsibility at Intuit, delivered a passionate and heartfelt keynote address at HCC'S Annual Susie Steiner Community Impact Award Breakfast. Dave concluded his impactful presentation with a simple but profound slide, "Together We Prosper." Together, we can provide prosperity and opportunity to all.

Conclusion References

Manyika, J., Bughin, J., Lind, S., Nottebohm, O., Poulter, D., Jauch, S., and Ramaswany, S. (2014) 'Global Flows in a Digital Age,' *McKinsey Global Institute*. Retrieved from https://www.mckinsey.com/business-functions/strategy-and-corporate-finance/our-insights/global-flows-in-a-digital-age#.

Afterword

America has long been metaphorically referred to as the "land of opportunity." It is a place where citizens and immigrants have diligently pursued the American Dream, which suggests that if you work hard, you will reach whatever goals you set. While this may have held true in the past, the structural inequities and increasing disparity among those who are privileged and those who are struggling just to survive make this profoundly improbable or impossible. The American Dream, once a goal to achieve, has now become a fantasy that many will never realize. The global pandemic has only further intensified this reality.

Education is the equalizer for social mobility, and entrepreneurship is the greatest driver of economic mobility. The authors eloquently provide a framework that connects the two. While the media glorifies tech entrepreneurs and giant corporations, the greatest drivers of job creation and economic recovery are actually small businesses. Organizations like NACCE and community colleges across the country empower everyday entrepreneurs to build new businesses as the engine for economic recovery — an inclusive and more equitable economic recovery.

John Duong
Founder & CEO
Kind Capital

About the Authors

Rebecca's Story of Purpose and Partnership with NACCE

Like many people, I never thought of myself as an entrepreneur. I just knew that I wanted to help other people through work with volunteer organizations. That desire led me to work as a campaign director for local United Ways in Ohio, Indiana, and Wisconsin in the late 1990s and early 2000s. I was drawn to the organization's interconnectedness of locally led United Ways working to serve people in communities in all 50 states, sharing a common brand, methodology, and mission. In the United Way system, ample room exists for creativity, cultural differences, and the engagement of diverse businesses, nonprofits, philanthropy, and government. Working together in a non-partisan way for the good of all in a cost-effective manner appealed to my sense of purpose and passion.

My desire to help others undoubtedly was sparked by my family. They embraced their Boston Irish heritage as descending proudly from immigrants who ascended to the middle class through hard work and public education. My father, David O'Brien is a sociologist who is forever fascinated with studying groups of people around the world. As my husband Mike and I raised our own family and encountered the joys of parenthood along with health and other challenges with our two wonderful children, we learned to work together and focus on our core strengths and what unites us as people who deeply love each other rather than our differences.

More than a decade later, I accepted the position as the executive director of the Rowan College at Burlington County Foundation in New Jersey. It opened my eyes to the power of community colleges to offer opportunity to people locally, and to amplify this impact regionally and nationally through a network of over 1,100 colleges. In my six years working at Rowan College, I mentored many students, similar to the student entrepreneurs profiled in this book who had life-changing experiences because they were taught and coached by caring, passionate professors like Beth Kerly and Andy Gold. These human connections and experiences fueled my desire to better understand how entrepreneurship, combined with workforce training and philanthropy, could ignite opportunities for people left behind. This passion and purpose helped sustain me through challenging times when funding for NACCE was in peril and when organizational changes that could have derailed my plans instead offered opportunities for innovation.

I became NACCE's leader in 2015 and the work continues to inspire and challenge me. My desire has always been to invite everyone to partner — other institutions, businesses, nonprofits, government, and philanthropy — and join one of NACCE's shovel-ready project initiatives or to plug in to a local community college or service agency that needs a mentor, speaker, advisor, or supporter. I have learned through the "crazy quilt" principle of effectuation that one future determinant in the success of NACCE will not be convincing others to partner with us, but rather finding the right partners that are aligned with our values and purpose. The NACCE culture encourages us to do what is etched onto my favorite coffee mug, "Create the things you wish existed."

Beth's Story of Purpose and Partnership

When I moved to Florida from Delaware, I knew that it was the time for me to make a career change. I held positions in public relations and marketing with a major power company and then with Big Brothers Big Sisters of Delaware. In both of these jobs, I was able to scratch the itch of service to others, from working on one of the first cause-based marketing programs for Delmarva Power and Light and serving as the United Way Co-chair, to volunteering as a Big Sister. When I arrived in Florida, I never anticipated the path that awaited me and how I would be able to fulfill my sense of purpose.

I began teaching as an adjunct instructor at Hillsborough Community College. The excitement of setting students on a path to a career was exhilarating. But when an opportunity to serve as the special assistant to then Governor Jeb Bush came along, I couldn't resist the call to serve. I was lucky to have a job that impacted the constituents of Florida in such a direct and meaningful way and work in an environment that valued creativity, innovation, and service to others. It was through this experience that I began to see the power of purpose and partnerships.

After leaving the governor's office in 2007, I had my daughter and took a year off from work, but I knew I had to get back into the classroom to feel that passion for helping others through education. Again, an opportunity presented itself, and I was hired as a full-time tenure-track faculty member at Hillsborough Community College. I never would have imagined 15 years ago that I would emerge as a thought leader on entrepreneurial education.

At the time I was hired, the word "entrepreneur" made me nervous. Just hearing it made me think of risk-takers who owned and operated their own businesses. And those awful business plans that I had to write in my MBA program — I had absolutely no desire to be an entrepreneur and did not think I had any entrepreneurial skills! I valued my tenure-track professor status and all the certainty it provided my family and me.

In 2012, after going to the college mailroom one afternoon, I came across a "save the date" postcard for an annual conference being hosted by NACCE. Of course, because I had no interest in entrepreneurship, I passed the card along to a new faculty member and co-author of this book, Andrew Gold, who I knew was a long-time entrepreneur turned educator and told him he should look into going to this event. He was thrilled at the notion of attending a conference about his two favorite subjects — entrepreneurship and education — and he proceeded to attend.

Andy came back completely jazzed about this amazing group of people who are innovative, action-oriented, and dedicated to community college students. He in turn energized me to investigate the possibility of rejuvenating a stale old entrepreneurship certificate program we had at the college. Together, we worked to change the internal culture at the college, launch not one, but three academic programs in entrepreneurship, and co-founded the InLab@HCC, which serves the college and greater community with services around entrepreneurship and innovation.

This journey has taken us seven years, during which we have pushed the status quo, engaged community members, taken an active role in NACCE, held large-scale events, and applied for and secured grants. Alone, neither of us could have accomplished building the InLab@HCC, launching the Everyday Entrepreneurship Venture Fund (EEVF) program, and supporting our beautifully diverse and growing group of entrepreneurs. We depend on each other for balance, creativity, and action. We live by the expression, "If you want to go fast, go alone; if you want to go far, go together." In the past two years, our work has accelerated rapidly. We have more support staff on our team, which allows us time to participate with the national EEVF steering committee and provide vision and leadership for NACCE.

I am a reluctant entrepreneur. Yet, with my partnership with Andy, we have built a nationally recognized entrepreneurship program that serves hundreds of students with a robust curriculum, mentorship, and funding opportunities. Without this partnership, we would not have been able impact our community, and even the world in which we live.

Andy's Story of Purpose and Partnership

Growing up in New York provided many valuable experiences, including the opportunity to work in the finance industry. After a 12-year career on Wall Street, I realized that there was a void in my life; I lacked a strong sense of professional purpose. My personal life was fulfilling. I was married to a wonderful wife, and blessed with two amazing sons, but a growing sense of wanting to do more professionally was taking hold. I learned many skills in the field of finance, but the work was not very rewarding. I would learn years later as a college professor how purposeful my working knowledge of finance could be in helping nascent entrepreneurs understand and absorb the complex waters of small business finance.

My quest for a more purposeful professional life began by getting involved as a community volunteer in New Rochelle, New York, as a youth baseball coach. Of course, I was able to spend a great deal of time with my two sons, and those experiences have been a long-lasting source of memories and laughter. I was also able to see how my volunteerism helped so many other children, and in some instances, their families.

After leaving the world of finance, I began my journey down a path of small business ownership. As a novice entrepreneur, I was most animated about the opportunity to be my own boss and potentially generate sufficient income for my family. That all changed one cold winter day. At that time, I owned a computer consulting business and was referred to a large nonprofit organization – Encore Community Services – based in St. Malachy's Church on West 49th Street in Manhattan. The organization was led by several Catholic nuns. Working with these amazing women reminded me about the power of purpose and the unconditional service to others who have no one to help lift them up.

"What happens to people who do not have someone willing to lend them a hand when no one else is willing to?" The question

haunted me and changed my life dramatically. I began to use effectuation long before I knew that term. I began to wonder what I currently had ("bird-in-hand") to help those crowded out from opportunity and resources.

I modified my business model so I could provide IT consultancy at a sharply discounted rate or for free to small nonprofit leaders that could not afford those services. I discovered something very interesting through that experience. My paying customers liked the fact that I was leveraging my profits for social good. In fact, it made my paying customers feel like they also were making the world a better place by simply hiring my business and paying for services rendered. I also learned that most people want to make the world a better place, but struggle with figuring out how to do that. Developing a for-profit social entrepreneurial business model enables a business owner to have a never-ending benefactor in paying customers. The more customers you acquire, the more impact you can have.

I took all of these life experiences and began to teach as an adjunct professor and learned how useful all of the mistakes I had made in my professional life could be for students. It was shortly thereafter that I applied for a full-time faculty position at Hillsborough Community College, and much to my surprise, was hired. There had been many other faculty positions that I had applied for that I was unsuccessful in securing. I have often wondered what would have happened had another school hired me. In all likelihood I would have never met my co-authors and professional partners, Beth and Rebecca. Without them, I would have never had the opportunity to be part of the co-creation of a dynamic entrepreneurship program with the capacity of scaling impact to help lift those who otherwise may have been left behind. My fortunate, but serendipitous partnership with NACCE has provided me with resources to work with a passionate and trusted group of colleagues with a shared enthusiasm for changemaking.

**CHANGEMAKERS
BOOKS**

Transform your life, transform *our* world. Changemakers
Books publishes books for people who seek to become positive,
powerful agents of change. These books inform, inspire, and
provide practical wisdom and skills to empower us to write the
next chapter of humanity's future.
www.changemakers-books.com

The *Resilience* Series

The Resilience Series is a collaborative effort by the authors of Changemakers Books in response to the 2020 coronavirus pandemic. Each concise volume offers expert advice and practical exercises for mastering specific skills and abilities. Our intention is that by strengthening your resilience, you can better survive and even thrive in a time of crisis.
www.resilience-books.com

Adapt and Plan for the New Abnormal – in the COVID-19 Coronavirus Pandemic
Gleb Tsipursky

Aging with Vision, Hope and Courage in a Time of Crisis
John C. Robinson

Connecting with Nature in a Time of Crisis
Melanie Choukas-Bradley

Going Within in a Time of Crisis
P. T. Mistlberger

Grow Stronger in a Time of Crisis
Linda Ferguson

Handling Anxiety in a Time of Crisis
George Hoffman

Navigating Loss in a Time of Crisis
Jules De Vitto

The Life-Saving Skill of Story
Michelle Auerbach

**Virtual Teams – Holding the Center When You Can't Meet
Face-to-Face**
Carlos Valdes-Dapena

Virtually Speaking – Communicating at a Distance
Tim Ward and Teresa Erickson

Current Bestsellers from Changemakers Books

Pro Truth
A Practical Plan for Putting Truth Back into Politics
Gleb Tsipursky and Tim Ward

How can we turn back the tide of post-truth politics, fake news, and misinformation that is damaging our democracy? In the lead up to the 2020 US Presidential Election, Pro Truth provides the answers.

An Antidote to Violence
Evaluating the Evidence
Barry Spivack and Patricia Anne Saunders

It's widely accepted that Transcendental Meditation can create peace for the individual, but can it create peace in society as a whole? And if it can, what could possibly be the mechanism?

Finding Solace at Theodore Roosevelt Island
Melanie Choukas-Bradley

A woman seeks solace on an urban island paradise in Washington D.C. through 2016–17, and the shock of the Trump election.

the bottom
a theopoetic of the streets
Charles Lattimore Howard

An exploration of homelessness fusing theology, jazz-verse and intimate storytelling into a challenging, raw and beautiful tale.

The Soul of Activism
A Spirituality for Social Change
Shmuly Yanklowitz

A unique examination of the power of interfaith spirituality to fuel the fires of progressive activism.

Future Consciousness
The Path to Purposeful Evolution
Thomas Lombardo

An empowering evolutionary vision of wisdom and the human mind to guide us in creating a positive future.

Preparing for a World that Doesn't Exist – Yet
Rick Smyre and Neil Richardson

This book is about an emerging Second Enlightenment and the capacities you will need to achieve success in this new, fast-evolving world.